jealousy

jealousy

Chapter 11

9

PAFF

I'M NOT TOO FAMILIAR WITH THE BUSINESS SIDE OF THINGS.

I'M COUNTING ON YOU TO HELP.

THE HAND ON MY SHOULDER WAS WARM AND FIRM.

I COULD FEEL HIS CONFIDENCE FLOWING INTO ME.

WELL, YOU WERE SCRUBBIN' THE SAME SPOT ON THAT TOILET FOR A GOOD TEN MINUTES STRAIGHT.

DAYS LATER, WHEN I FINALLY FOUND THE COURAGE TO ASK HIM HOW HE KNEW I HAD A SUGGESTION, HE SAID...

...AND THEN LAUGHED.

HE WAS A MASTER AT READING PEOPLE.

HE WANDERED THE STREETS WITHOUT BODYGUARDS FOR A REASON... SO HE COULD GET A FEEL FOR THE DESIRES OF THE PEOPLE AND HOW THAT REFLECTED ON LOCAL PRICES.

IT ALL MAKES SENSE. ...

THAT'S WHEN IT HIT ME.

UH, WHOA. HOLD ON. WHAT'S WITH THE "YOUNG MASTER" STUFF?

I HAVE BEEN UNSPEAKABLY RUDE, AND I BEG YOUR FORGIVENESS.

PLEASE. I WILL DO ANYTHING FOR A CHANCE TO REDEEM MYSELF.

PLEASE! ALLOW ME TO CALL YOU THAT!

NO WAY! IT'S TACKY AND GROSS.

WAH HA HA! C'MON, BOSS! WHAT'S SO WRONG WITH IT?

I WAS INTENSELY ASHAMED FOR BELIEVING SO EASILY IN THE RUMORS.

YOUNG MASTER.

GEH.

WHY ARE *YOU* HERE?

BECAUSE I CAME TO GET YOU. GET IN.

WHAT?

YOU'LL GET DISTRACTED AND TURN A TEN-MINUTE TRIP INTO AN HOUR-LONG DETOUR.

I CAN MAKE IT TO A COFFEE SHOP WITHOUT A BABY-SITTER.

IN. NOW. THE BOSS IS WAITING.

13

TRACKING JUST MONTHLY SHIFTS MEANT I COULD GET IT DONE QUICK WITH A LITTLE FOCUS.

I'M UP ALMOST ALL NIGHT ANYWAY.

SEE HOW THIS MOVES HERE? FOLLOW THE LINE AND...

GOING INTO DETAIL WILL TAKE FOREVER, SO I'LL KEEP IT SHORT. THERE'S A PATTERN.

IT FOLLOWS RULES YOU CAN PREDICT.

HAH! DON'T BE STUPID. WITH AS GOOD AS THE ECONOMY IS RIGHT NOW, IT'S HARD TO BELIEVE IT'D CRASH THAT FAST.

PFFT!

INTERESTING. THE GRAPH DIPS THERE, SO YOU'RE SAYING THE ECONOMY WILL DIP TOO?

YEP!

TA-DAH! THE JAPANESE ECONOMY IS DOOMED! SOMETIME NEXT YEAR THE BOTTOM WILL FALL OUT.

KABOOM!

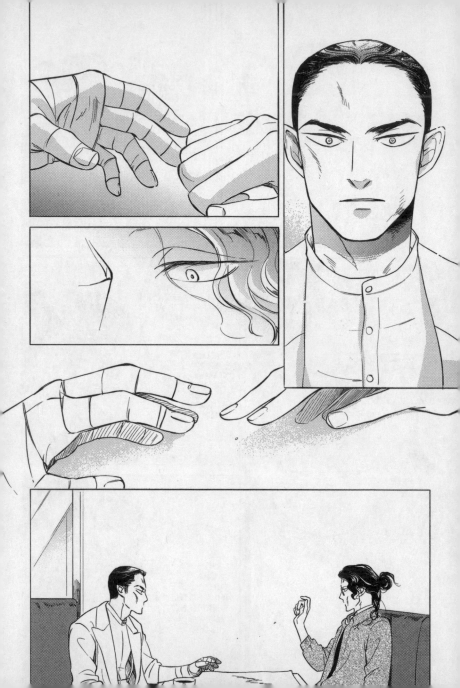

THEY SAID IF YOU CAN'T MAKE IT YOURSELF TO AT LEAST SEND MA'AM AND YOUNG TATSUYUKI IN YOUR STEAD.

THEY'VE REQUESTED THAT YOU VISIT TO EXPLAIN YOUR ABSENCE FROM THE SECOND HEAD'S RELEASE PARTY.

HAH! THAT'S A NICE WAY OF SAYIN' "WE'RE TAKING 'EM HOSTAGE."

FEH! PAIN IN THE ASS.

HUH?

IT'S FINE. ENJOY YOUR COFFEE.

BUT, BOSS, YOU MUSTN'T...

YOU TAKE UICHI HOME.

ALL RIGHT, ALL RIGHT. I'LL GO.

JINGLE

JANGLE

26

CAFE ROMANTIC

VRRRM

27

32

34

WHEN I ASKED IF HE COULD TEACH ME, HE PUT THE SHOVEL DOWN AND LET ME COME IN.

IT LOOKED LIKE HE HAD BEEN SITTING IN THERE PLAYING BY HIMSELF FOR A LONG TIME.

...AND HE SAID HE WOULDN'T MIND LEAVING IT TO ME.

I LET HIM RAMBLE ON FOR A WHILE BEFORE BRINGING UP THE LAND THING...

STUBBORN, CRANKY OLD MEN USUALLY WANT TO TEACH A THING OR TWO TO US YOUNGSTERS, RIGHT?

HEY, ASODA?

36

41

jealousy
Chapter 12

48

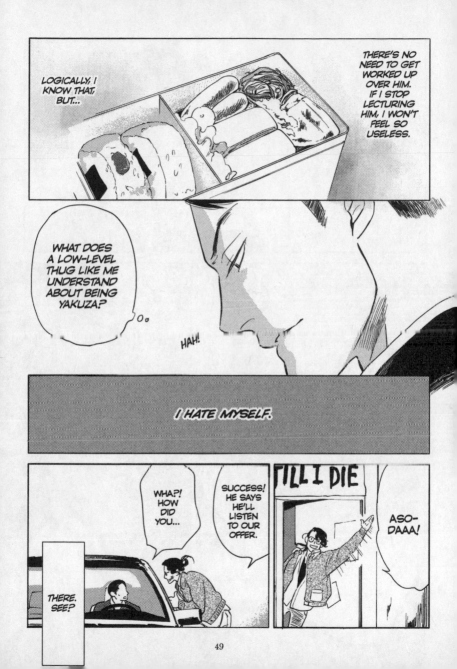

YOU CAN TAKE THE CREDIT FOR THIS IF YOU WANT.

HAH!

I WAS SO SHOCKED ALL I COULD DO WAS PARROT HIM LIKE AN IDIOT.

I...I CAN?

IS HE GIVING ME HANDOUTS OUT OF PURE PITY NOW?

HEH HEH HEH HEH.

YEAH, TOTALLY! WE'RE FRIENDS, RIGHT? LET'S BOTH DO OUR BEST FOR THE GUY WE LOVE, 'KAY?

WHAT IS HE SAYING?

THERE'S NOTHING I CAN DO BUT LAUGH.

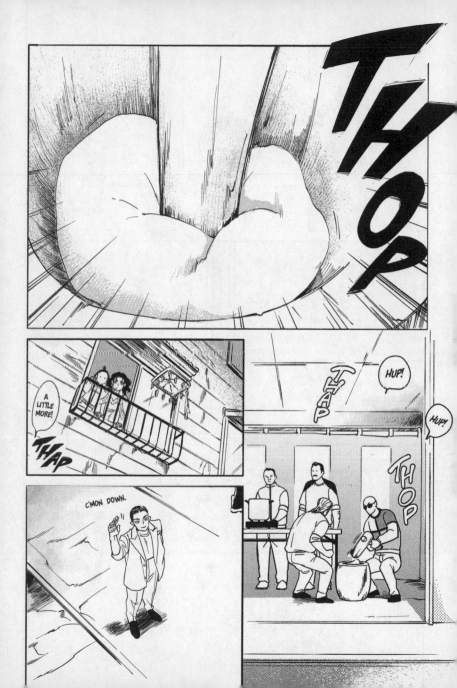

58

BUT WHEN YOU SAY "GO," WHAT YOU REALLY MEAN IS "STAY."

UGH. YOU ARE SUCH A PAIN IN THE ASS. YOU NEVER DO WHAT I ASK YOU TO.

YEAH. YOU WERE ALWAYS A CONFUSING GUY, BUT NOW YOU'RE EVEN MORE SO.

Y'KNOW? YOU REALLY HAVE CHANGED.

I HAVE?

AHA HA HA.

HE JUST MIGHT'VE.

WELL?

DO YOU WANT ME TO KILL YOU?!

ARE YOU SURE UICHI HASN'T PUT YOU UNDER SOME KIND OF HYPNOSIS OR SOMETHING?

ARE YOU OKAY?

CRAP.

HOW ABOUT WE HAVE AN AFFAIR.

I LET ON ENOUGH I'D MAKE HIM WORRY.

GETTING ASKED IF I'M OKAY IS AN INSULT.

GAWD, YOU'RE SO SERIOUS.

I KID, I KID!

AHA HA HA!

W-W-W-WHAT?!

M-MA'AM! WE COULDN'T!

HEY, ASODA?

I'M NOT WEAK ENOUGH TO LET THIS LITTLE THING GET ME DOWN, Y'KNOW.

69

73

...WOMEN ARE LIFE.

ON THE OTHER HAND...

AND LIFE IS BEAUTIFUL.

LOOKING AT ASAMI, I TRULY BELIEVE THAT.

YANK

AKITORA?

OW...

BUT THIS MAN, WHO SMELLS OF YOUTH AND DEATH...

...HE STILL HAS EVERYTHING I THOUGHT I HAD TO THROW AWAY.

HUG

Chapter 13

jealousy
Chapter 13

DID MR. MATSUMI SAY WHAT HIS BUSINESS WAS TODAY?

HE MENTIONED HE'D RECEIVED A CALL FROM A MR. MIYAKAWA...

...AND THAT HE'D DISCUSS THE REST WITH YOU PERSONALLY.

AH. GIVEN THE TIMING, I'M BETTING IT'LL BE A DISCUSSION ABOUT SOME GOLD BARS.

QUIT MAKING EVERYTHING YOUR FAULT.

THIS IS MY FAULT, SIR. I DIDN'T INVESTIGATE THE TARGET AS THOROUGHLY AS I SHOULD'VE.

NOBODY CAN FULLY GRASP SOMEONE'S UNDERWORLD CONNECTIONS.

I WAS THINKING HE'D MAKE A MAD DASH STRAIGHT FOR THE COPS AFTER I WALKED OUT THE DOOR...

...BANGING ON THE POLICE BOX SHOUTING "THE YAKUZA STOLE MY DIRTY MONEY!"

STILL, TO THINK THAT ACADEMIC-TURNED-LAWYER WAS ALREADY FRIENDS WITH THE YAKUZA.

LAUGH.

LEAN

HUH?! ER! SORRY, SIR!

...

THERE'S INSTANT CURRY AT THE OFFICE, RIGHT?

DAMN IT... I MISSED OUT ON LUNCH TOO.

GRGL

OH?

YOU SEEM RATHER CALM, SIR, CONSIDERING.

TRUE.

STILL, AT TIMES THERE'S NO END TO IT.

THAT'S THE DUTY I'VE BEEN GIVEN, SIR.

YOU SURE *YOU* AREN'T TOO NERVOUS?

YOU ALWAYS TRY TO ENVISION EVERY LAST THING THAT COULD GO WRONG SO YOU CAN PREPARE FOR IT.

101

I PRESUME YOU'RE HERE TO INQUIRE ABOUT CERTAIN GOLD BARS?

THAT I AM. HE CAME CRYING TO OUR DOORSTEP FIRST THING NEW YEAR'S.

HOWEVER, AS WE ARE TECHNICALLY ACQUAINTED WITH HIM, WE DO AT LEAST NEED TO KEEP UP APPEARANCES. THAT'S WHY I DROPPED BY TODAY.

FROM WHERE WE STAND, THE GOLD STILL BELONGS TO THE OYAMATO SYNDICATE, NO MATTER WHICH PATH IT TOOK TO REACH US. MR. MIYAKAWA'S DIRTY MONEY MEANS LITTLE TO US.

NO, NO. DON'T LET IT BOTHER YOU.

I'M SORRY MY LACK OF KNOWLEDGE HAS CAUSED YOU ALL THIS EXTRA EFFORT.

NOT IN THE LEAST. I'LL MAKE UP SOME EXCUSE TO PLACATE HIM.

THEN YOU WON'T ASK ME TO RETURN IT?

PERHAPS THAT'S THE WAY IT IS BETWEEN FATHER AND SON. I WOULDN'T KNOW.
BUT YOU MADE A DELIBERATE CHOICE TO ENTER THIS FIELD, AND YOU'RE GOING OUT OF YOUR WAY TO HAMPER HIM.
IN THIS LINE OF WORK, ONE'S BOSS IS AS ONE'S FATHER. AND ONE'S FATHER IS AS GOD.
THIS LATE REBELLIOUS PHASE OF YOURS SEEMS A TAD MUCH, TO BE HONEST.
I KNOW YOU AREN'T THE KIND OF FOOL WHO WISHES TO GO SWIMMING IN THE BAY.
SO WHAT IN THE WORLD ARE YOU HOPING TO ACHIEVE?
I'M QUITE CURIOUS.

121

RIING

KVK

HELLO! THANK YOU FOR CALLING YAMASAN BROKERAGE.

MR. SUZUKI, HELLO! IT'S ASODA. HM? YOU AREN'T MR. SUZUKI?

OH, I'M SO SORRY! I MUST'VE DIALED THE WRONG EXTENSION. GUESS I HAVEN'T HAD ENOUGH COFFEE YET.

HA HA HA!

I'M SORRY, AH... WHAT WAS YOUR NAME AGAIN? MR. KOGA?

RIGHT. I APOLOGIZE FOR THE BOTHER, MR. KOGA.

123

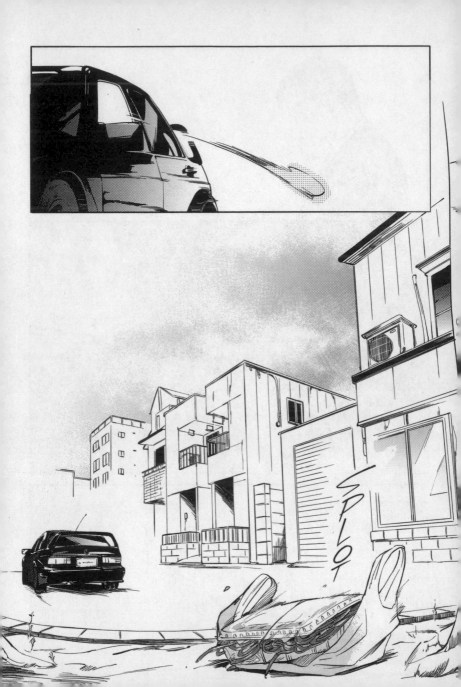

K
C
H
A
K

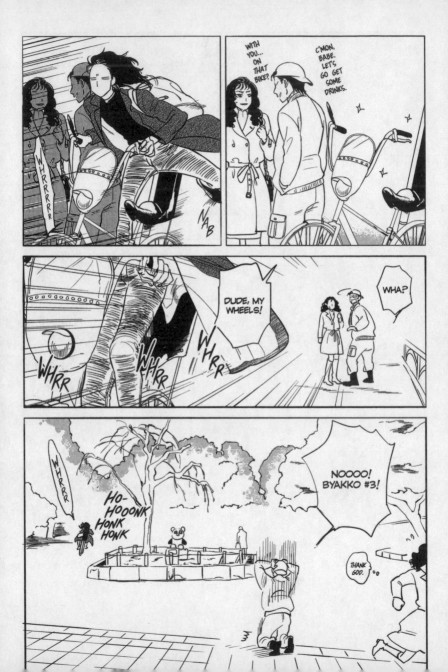

140

142

143

144

148

149

GLUG
GLUG
GLUG
GLUG

BUT I'M HUNGRY. I SAID I'D BE FINE WITH WATER, BUT IF YOU'RE GIVING IT TO ME FOR FREE, I'LL TAKE IT.

UH, THIS MAY SOUND ODD COMING FROM ME, BUT PERHAPS YOU SHOULD SHOW A LITTLE MORE CAUTION?

I'M VERY AWARE OF THE EXPRESSION I MADE A MOMENT AGO.

MNCH MNCH

BUUURP

THUNK

BURP

MY WHUH?

YOU REALLY CAN'T RESIST YOUR IMMEDIATE DESIRES, CAN YOU?

KRNCH
KRNCH

CAN'T HEAR YOU OVER MY CHEWING.

156

159

YOU LOOK A LOT BETTER THAN YOU DID LAST I SAW YOU, THOUGH.

NEVER HAD ANYBODY SO STRICT ABOUT HOW I'M SUPPOSED TO CLEAN STUFF.

I'M NOTHIN' BUT BRUISES.

YES, SIR. GETTIN' THE RIGHT WAY TO DO THINGS BEAT INTO ME, THAT'S FOR SURE.

YEAH.

YOU'RE HAPPY?

SO I, UH...

YES, SIR, YOU BET. THE OWNER HERE DOESN'T JUDGE ME BECAUSE OF MY HERITAGE.

YES, SIR.

STAY ON YOUR TOES, THOUGH. THE MOST DANGEROUS TIME IS WHEN YOU'VE FULLY SETTLED INTO THE JOB.

DON'T GET COMPLACENT. REMEMBER THE BOSS'S GENEROSITY IN TAKING YOU IN AND BE SURE TO REPAY HIM.

THAT'S THE BEST DUTY TO GIVE THOSE ON THE BOTTOM RUNG.

FIRST, YOU BEGIN BY TRAINING AND DISCIPLINING YOURSELF.

164

165

HE TOLD ME A BROKER WOULD NEVER MANIPULATE A TRADE OUTSIDE OF THEIR CLIENT'S WISHES. THERE'S NO BENEFIT TO DOING SO, AND IT DAMAGES THEIR CLIENT'S TRUST IN THEM.

I DISCUSSED THE MATTER WITH AN ACQUAINTANCE OF MINE WHO'S A STOCK-BROKER.

HE WAS SO INSISTENT THAT HE HADN'T MADE THE WRONG DECISION, DESPITE THE TRADE FAILING, THAT IT MADE ME CURIOUS.

R I I I I P

AN INTERESTING ANSWER, BUT I SUSPECTED THERE WAS MORE TO IT. I FLIPPED THE QUESTION AROUND.

I ASKED HIM IF THEY WOULD CONSIDER DOING SO IF THEIR FAMILY OR LOVED ONES WERE THREATENED.

HE SAID THAT, IN THAT CASE, IT WAS NOT UNTHINK-ABLE.

THAT'S A TECHNIQUE THOSE IN OUR FIELD ARE KNOWN TO RESORT TO, AFTER ALL. UNSURPRIS-INGLY, HIS ANSWER CHANGED.

167

THAT RECKLESS, SEDUCTIVE YOUNG MAN.

THE YOUNG SIR'S RECENT REBELLIOUS ATTITUDE.

THAT TOLD ME ALL THAT I NEEDED.

YOUR RECENT IMPATIENCE.

VERY IMPRESSIVE, SIR.

I THINK I HAVE MOST OF IT PIECED TOGETHER NOW.

169

I, TOO, STARTED OUT CLEANING TOILETS WITH MY BARE HANDS.

THE POWER OF SEEDS

TOK

TIK

TIK

TOK

Good Sign

HUP.

GUESS
HE'S
NOT
COMING
BACK
TODAY
EITHER.

171

SNIF

I HAD A
DREAM.

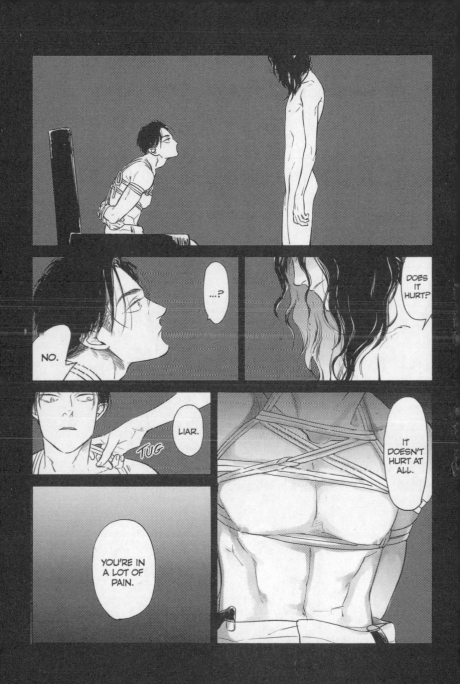

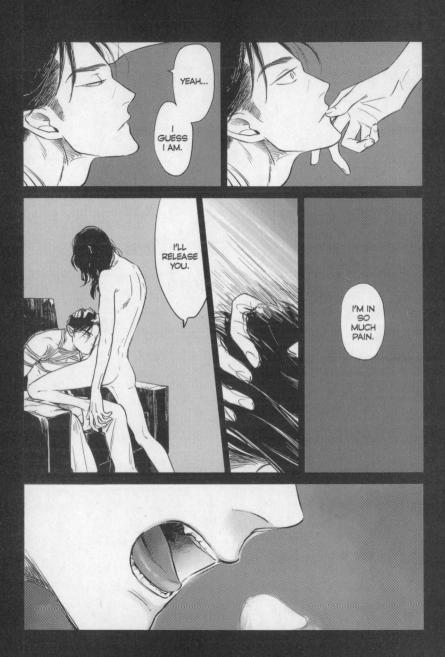

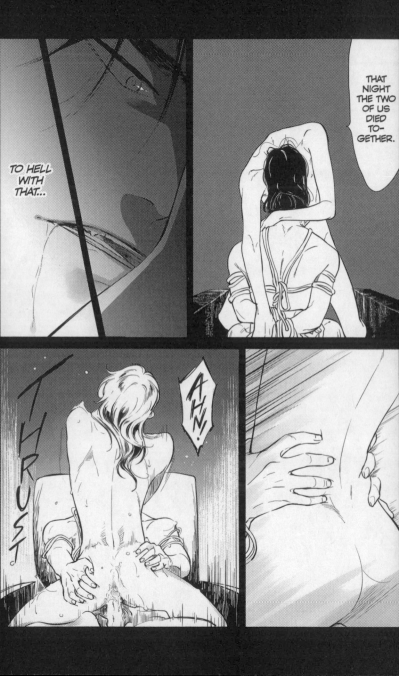

YOU ARE A NIGHT-MARE...

...UICHI.

End

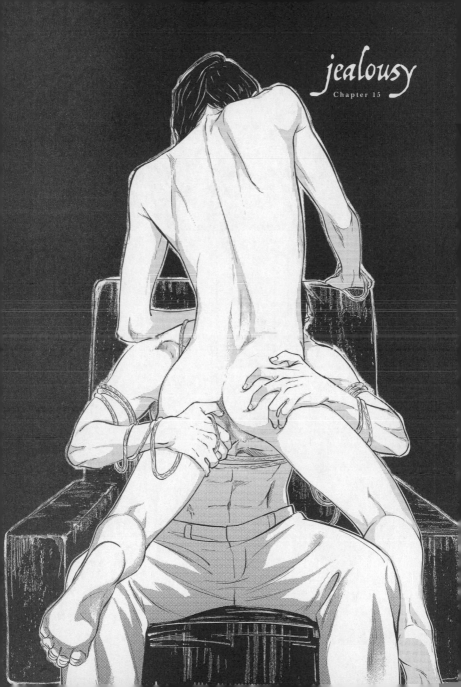

jealousy

Chapter 15

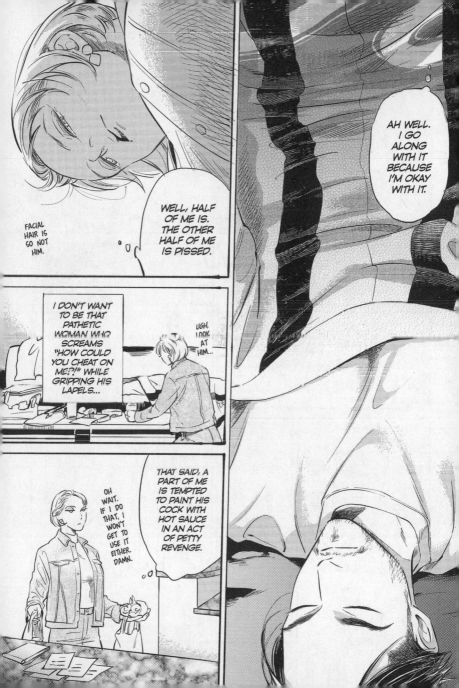

184

SOME YAKUZA I'D NEVER MET BEFORE DEMANDED I TURN YOUR SELL ORDER INTO A BUY!

IF I DIDN'T, HE SAID THERE WAS NO TELLING WHAT WOULD HAPPEN TO MY KIDS!

YOUR KIDS ARE IMPORTANT TO YOU, HUH?

PAFF

THAT'S THE WAY IT SHOULD BE.

SNIFL

HE WOULDN'T LET ME OUT OF THE CAR UNTIL I SWORE I WOULD DO IT. I-I WAS SO SCARED I...

BUT, MR. KOGA? YOU AREN'T CUT OUT TO BE A STOCKBROKER.

I SUGGEST YOU QUIT, OPEN UP A LITTLE BUSINESS, AND SPEND TIME WITH YOUR KIDS.

192

193

196

197

198

201

FINE.
I DID IT.

I DON'T
GET WHY
HE WAS
EITHER.

MR. KOGA
TOLD ME
HE HAD NO
IDEA WHY HE
WAS BEING
THREATENED,
BUT HE HAD
TO GO ALONG
WITH IT FOR
HIS KIDS'
SAKE.

DIDN'T
WE JUST
GET DONE
SAYING
WE WERE
FRIENDS?!

WHY GO
THAT FAR
JUST TO
SCREW ME
OVER?!

207

209

214

215

...HE DECIDED TO GET A TATTOO.

THE DAY ASODA DEDICATED HIS LIFE TO HIS BOSS...

UM?!

I DON'T HAVE ANY TATTOOS.

TOO STUFFY AND TRADITIONAL.

ER, IF YOU DON'T MIND, COULD I USE YOURS AS A REFERENCE FOR THE DETAILS ON MY DESIGN?

REALLY? GOOD FOR YOU.

BOSS. I TOOK THE LIBERTY OF GETTING THE OUTLINE OF A TIGER-THEMED TATTOO ON MY BACK.

MY WHA?

SLURP

YOU CRYING, SONNY?

IT BECAME A BITTER MEMORY OF YOUTHFUL ENTHUSIASM GONE WRONG.

NO...

SPECIAL THANKS: LYLE HIROSHI SAXON [YOUTUBE CHANNEL: LYLE HIROSHI SAXON]; MASATO SEKIZAKI

About the Author

Scarlet Beriko began her professional manga career in 2010 and has since gone on to create many manga in the BL genre, including *Jackass!* and a constellation of related works—*Minori no Te, Fourth Generation Head: Tatsuyuki Oyamato*, and *Jealousy*. She has also published tutorials on drawing manga. Her birthday is March 21, and her blood type is A or O.

Jealousy
Volume 3
SuBLime Manga Edition

Story and Art by **Scarlet Beriko**

Translation—**Adrienne Beck**
Touch-Up Art and Lettering—**E.K. Weaver**
Cover and Graphic Design—**Julian [JR] Robinson**
Editor—**Jennifer LeBlanc**

© 2019 Beriko SCARLET
Originally published in Japan in 2019 by Shinshokan Co., Ltd.

Original Japanese Cover Design—Tomohiro Kusume (arcoinc)

Printed in the U.S.A.

Published by SuBLime Manga
P.O. Box 77010
San Francisco, CA 94107

10 9 8 7 6 5 4 3 2 1
First printing, January 2021

www.SuBLimeManga.com

JACKASS!

STORY AND ART BY **SCARLET BERIKO**

WHEN THE PANTY HOSE GO ON, ALL BETS ARE OFF BETWEEN THESE BEST GUY FRIENDS!

Practical Keisuke's incredibly handsome best friend Masayuki has always rubbed him just a little bit the wrong way. Maybe it's because Masayuki is rich, carefree, and so stunningly handsome that he can, and does, have any girl he wants? But one day, when Keisuke accidentally wears his older sister's panty hose to gym class, it's suddenly his hot friend who's doing the rubbing… on Keisuke's panty hose-clad legs! Has he unwittingly unleashed a secret fetish that will change their relationship forever?

 MATURE

SuBLime
SuBLimeManga.com

Finder
DELUXE EDITION

PAIN AND PLEASURE COLLIDE when a sophisticated underworld boss crosses paths with a naive photographer hell-bent on bringing him down!

**STORY AND ART BY
AYANO YAMANE**

This deluxe edition includes never-before-released material as well as a double-sided color insert and special cover treatment!

Photographer Akihito Takaba takes on a risky assignment trying to document the illegal activities of the Japanese underworld. When he captures its leader—the handsome, enigmatic Ryuichi Asami—in the cross-hairs of his viewfinder, Takaba's world is changed forever.

A collection of masterful, sensual stories by Kou Yoneda!

NightS

Story & Art by KOU YONEDA

In the title story, Masato Karashima is a "transporter," a man paid to smuggle anything from guns to drugs to people. When he's hired by yakuza gang member Masaki Hozumi, he finds himself attracted to the older man, and what starts out as a business transaction quickly spirals into a cat-and-mouse game of lust and deception. In "Emotion Spectrum," a high-school student tries to be a good wingman for a classmate, with an unexpected result, while "Reply" is told from the alternating perspectives of an emotionally reserved salesman and the shy mechanic who's in love with him.

SUBLIME

Downloading is as easy as:

1

2

3

SUBLIME

Your Toys Love Boys' Love

Own your SuBLime book as a convenient PDF document that is downloadable to the following devices:

- ♥ Computer
- ♥ Kindle™
- ♥ NOOK™
- ♥ iPad™, iPhone™, and iPod Touch™
- ♥ Any device capable of reading a PDF document

Praise for EXPERIENCING THE SPIRIT

Experiencing the Spirit is must reading. It can heal and change whole communities of faith. Robert Heidler contends that we should live every moment sustained by the energies of the Holy Spirit. Walking in cadence with the Spirit is the best way—the only way—to overcome the gravitational pull of the flesh.

JOE ALDRICH
PRESIDENT, MULTNOMAH BIBLE COLLEGE, PORTLAND, OREGON

Experiencing the Spirit is an outstanding book. Robert Heidler's excellent presentation of the many facets of the Holy Spirit is done in a remarkable manner that will bring insight to those who doubt the existence or need of the Holy Spirit today; instruct those who have never experienced Him; and bless the new believer and the mature Spirit-filled Christian. As a pastor, I am pleased to have available to me and my flock a book that speaks the truth, is scripturally based and presented with personal testimonies of the presence and power of the Holy Spirit in our world today.

JOHN M. BENEFIEL
FOUNDER AND SENIOR PASTOR, CHURCH ON THE ROCK
OKLAHOMA CITY, OKLAHOMA

Robert Heidler's theological foundation at Dallas Theological Seminary combined with his own personal encounters with the Holy Spirit provide an excellent context for this book. The Church today needs teachers with such passion for Jesus, responsible exegetical skills and a genuine life flow in the Holy Spirit. We also need more books like *Experiencing the Spirit*.

MIKE BICKLE
SENIOR PASTOR, METRO CHRISTIAN FELLOWSHIP
VICE PRESIDENT, GRACE TRAINING CENTER OF KANSAS CITY, MISSOURI

Praise for EXPERIENCING THE SPIRIT

Robert Heidler's book clearly describes the power available to ordinary people to see tremendous change in their lives through the work of the Holy Spirit. Heidler's instructions on learning to hear the voice of God are simple enough to draw even young Christians into a dynamic interaction with the Spirit of God. The study guide at the end of the book will enable students of the Word to examine each precept in depth. This book is a must read for those who desire a greater flow of the gifts of the Holy Spirit and who are hungry for more of God's manifest presence.

MARY A. GLAZIER
FOUNDER AND PRESIDENT, WINDWALKERS INTERNATIONAL
ANCHORAGE, ALASKA

This outstanding book will serve as a bridge-builder in the Body of Christ. Too often we have argued over the Spirit's ministry and thereby limited Him in His ongoing work in the Church. I especially liked Robert's analysis of the Holy Spirit's work in the individual believer's life as: (1) indwelling; and (2) empowering. The author's outstanding teaching gifts shine through this entire volume. I do not know of a better contemporary book about the Spirit.

JIM HODGES
PRESIDENT, FEDERATION OF MINISTERS AND CHURCHES, INC.
DUNCANVILLE, TEXAS

Robert Heidler has given us valuable insight into God's purpose for giving the Holy Spirit to His people. *Experiencing the Spirit* will help you to know intimately the full life of Christ in your life. It will also help you to be instrumental in ministering the Holy Spirit to others. Bless you, Robert, for your commitment to Christ and His Church.

BILL HAMON
AUTHOR OF *APOSTLES, PROPHETS AND THE COMING MOVES OF GOD*
PRESIDENT AND FOUNDER, CHRISTIAN INTERNATIONAL MINISTRIES
TALLAHASSEE, FLORIDA

Praise for EXPERIENCING THE SPIRIT

Robert Heidler's book *Experiencing the Spirit* draws the reader into
an intimate encounter with the Holy Spirit. For everyone who wants
a deeper, richer relationship with the Lord, this book is a must!

CINDY JACOBS
COFOUNDER, GENERALS OF INTERCESSION
COLORADO SPRINGS, COLORADO

There is not another book as needed today in the Body of Christ
as *Experiencing the Spirit*. Not only has Robert Heidler experienced
the Spirit, but he communicates the principles of relationship
better than anyone I know. Read, study and meditate through these
principles. You will be empowered and equipped in a new way.

CHUCK D. PIERCE
DIRECTOR, WORLD PRAYER CENTER
COLORADO SPRINGS, COLORADO

Experiencing the Spirit is a refreshing, life-giving book! Not simply
theory or theology but totally biblical, it will whet your appetite for
the reality and power of the Holy Spirit. You will settle for nothing less
than to trust Him, cooperate with Him and enjoy Him to the utmost!

MARY AUDREY RAYCROFT
TEACHER, AUTHOR, SPEAKER, LEADERSHIP TEAM MEMBER
TORONTO AIRPORT CHRISTIAN FELLOWSHIP
TORONTO, ONTARIO, CANADA

One of the most important books ever written about the person, the
ministry and the power of the Holy Spirit. And with rivers of revival
flowing to all corners of the world, it couldn't have come at a better time!
Robert Heidler has given us a masterful study of the Spirit and the Word.

DUTCH SHEETS
AUTHOR OF *THE RIVER OF GOD*
PASTOR, SPRINGS HARVEST FELLOWSHIP
COLORADO SPRINGS, COLORADO

Praise for EXPERIENCING THE SPIRIT

Robert Heidler is an insightful biblical thinker who brings clarity to the person and purpose of the Holy Spirit. *Experiencing the Spirit* will create within you the desire to know the Holy Spirit in the fullness of God's intended purposes for His people and His kingdom.

JEAN STEFFENSON
FOUNDER, NATIVE AMERICAN RESOURCE NETWORK
CASTLE ROCK, COLORADO

Every true believer sows precious seed in God's kingdom. Robert Heidler sows seed for the end-time harvest—seed both precious and necessary. As Robert writes, "Most Christians have little concept of the resources God has given us." Beyond my feeble concepts exists a deep hunger for the things of the Spirit and for the Spirit Himself. Thank you for this timely word from the heart of King Jesus!

FRED SUUGIINA BRODIN, LITT.D.
SERVANT TO 1ST NATION'S PEOPLES
FAIRBANKS, ALASKA

During this season of renewal and revival, hungry hearts are searching for a fresh encounter with the Lord. *Experiencing the Spirit* provides a solid biblical foundation and practical instruction for a life characterized by the supernatural. It's a marvelous way to lead believers into a life empowered by the Holy Spirit!

BARBARA WENTROBLE
PRESIDENT, WENTROBLE CHRISTIAN MINISTRIES
DUNCANVILLE, TEXAS

Praise for EXPERIENCING THE SPIRIT

Robert Heidler is one of the most anointed teaching "gifts" given by God to the Body of Christ today. I wholeheartedly endorse *Experiencing the Spirit* as a rich resource of wisdom and practical helps on developing a vibrant, living relationship with the Spirit of God.

WAYNE WILKS, JR., PH.D.

INTERNATIONAL DIRECTOR, MESSIANIC JEWISH BIBLE INSTITUTE
ODESSA, UKRAINE AND BUDAPEST, HUNGARY

God's plan is to empower His people through the Spirit. Robert Heidler shows us how to move from simply taking a theoretical or theological position on the Holy Spirit to experiencing Him as a person through His manifest presence and power. Read this book and you will not only be changed but also begin to release the Holy Spirit's power and presence to those around you. I highly recommend it.

BARBARA J. YODER

SENIOR COPASTOR, SHEKINAH CHRISTIAN CHURCH
ANN ARBOR, MICHIGAN

EXPERIENCING THE SPIRIT

DEVELOPING

A LIVING RELATIONSHIP

WITH THE HOLY SPIRIT

EXPERIENCING
*the*SPIRIT

Robert Heidler

Renew

A Division of Gospel Light
Ventura, California, U.S.A.

\\\ | / / PUBLISHED BY REGAL BOOKS
━┌ᕦᒣ╗━ FROM GOSPEL LIGHT
~└┘~ VENTURA, CALIFORNIA, U.S.A.
Regal PRINTED IN THE U.S.A.

Regal Books is a ministry of Gospel Light, a Christian publisher dedicated to serving the local church. We believe God's vision for Gospel Light is to provide church leaders with biblical, user-friendly materials that will help them evangelize, disciple and minister to children, youth and families.

It is our prayer that this Regal book will help you discover biblical truth for your own life and help you meet the needs of others. May God richly bless you.

For a free catalog of resources from Regal Books/Gospel Light, please call your Christian supplier or contact us at 1-800-4-GOSPEL *or* www.regalbooks.com.

Cover Design by Kevin Keller
Interior Design by Robert Williams
Edited by David Webb

Library of Congress Cataloging-in-Publication Data
Heidler, Robert D., 1948–
Experiencing the Spirit / Robert D. Heidler.
        p.   cm.
ISBN 0-8307-2361-7 (trade)
1. Holy Spirit. 2. Gifts, Spiritual. 3. Experience (Religion)
I. Title.
BT121.2.H365 1999   98-44571
231'.3—dc21   CIP

    7 8 9 10 11 12 13 14 15 16 17 18 19 / 11 10 09 08 07

Rights for publishing this book in other languages are contracted by Gospel Light Worldwide, the international nonprofit ministry of Gospel Light. Gospel Light Worldwide also provides publishing and technical assistance to international publishers dedicated to producing Sunday School and Vacation Bible School curricula and books in the languages of the world. For additional information, visit www.gospellightworldwide.org; write to Gospel Light Worldwide, P.O. Box 3875, Ventura, CA 93006; or send an e-mail to info@gospellightworldwide.org.

This book is lovingly dedicated

To my wonderful wife, Linda, who has stood by my side through good times and bad.

And to Chuck Pierce, the most spiritual man I know, who has lifted my feet from the miry clay on many occasions, and has helped me begin to understand the things of the Spirit.

CONTENTS

FOREWORD

We live in one of the most exciting times in the history of the Church. These are days of divine connections. During these times, we must know with whom we are co-laboring in harvest. I am thankful that the Lord brought Robert Heidler into my life twelve years ago.

My wife and I had just moved to Denton, Texas, to work with a mission organization that ministered into the former Soviet Union. We were both seeking something different in our form of worship. We had been members of a major denomination all of our adult lives, and while that was wonderful for one season of our life together, we were being led to seek a new depth, demonstration and intimacy with the Holy Spirit.

I was told that a Dallas Theological Seminary graduate, who pastored a church in this north Texas city, had just received a new infilling of the Holy Spirit and that this experience was causing a "stir" in the religious community. I watched the Lord divinely lead my family to the church where this pastor, Robert Heidler, was teaching. I immediately saw in him a depth of love for the Word of God and a hunger for the Holy Spirit that I had not seen in anyone else in the entire area. It was a divine connection—not just with this wonderful scholar of the Word, but with the Holy Spirit of God!

Today the Holy Spirit is calling His people to experience new dimensions of His presence. Indeed a window of opportunity is forming for us to enter into a dimension of power most Christians have never experienced. Jesus is now moving us into a day when we will do the "greater works" that He predicted. The Third Person of the Trinity manifesting in us will be the key that allows each member of the Body of Christ to reach his or her destiny in the days ahead. Old distinctions and labels that separated us in the past will no longer be recognizable as men and women from many backgrounds press in to a new dimension of fullness. Through this move of the Spirit and through the prayer movement and the restoration of prophets and apostles to His Church, God is preparing a people who will witness the ingathering of the great end-time harvest.

For many Christians, however, the realm of the Spirit can be bewildering. Many who sincerely desire to move forward in the Lord are hindered by a lack of understanding and weighed down by unanswered questions. *Experiencing the Spirit* is designed to be a primer, a kind of "Holy Spirit 101" that answers these questions and serves as an introduction to the ministries of the Spirit. But Robert Heidler doesn't just initiate men and women into the workings of the Holy Spirit; he establishes them with ministry techniques for the future. A key book for one of the greatest transitions the Church has known, *Experiencing the Spirit* will enable you to move past questions and misconceptions and enter into the reality of an experiential walk with the Helper who will assist each of us in making that transition—the Holy Spirit.

Experiencing the Spirit is not a theological textbook, but a practical manual in how to operate in the things of the Spirit. Robert Heidler provides easy-to-understand explanations and clear, biblical teaching on such issues as receiving the Spirit's power, hearing the voice of God, receiving and exercising spiritual gifts, recognizing the Spirit's manifest presence and understanding how to have a relationship and communion with a holy God within us. With illustrations and real-life testimonies that encourage you to seek the reality of the Spirit's work in your own life, this book is an excellent starting point to deepen your walk with the Lord and grow in your ability to serve and demonstrate Him effectively.

Experiencing the Spirit is a collection of wonderful teachings and activations, communicated in profound, yet simple ways that will launch you on a new journey of experience. Just as *Experiencing God* by Henry Blackaby caused many throughout the Body of Christ to be renewed in their knowledge of a holy God and His ways, this book will give you a clear understanding of the Person and work of the Holy Spirit and lead you into intimate relationship with Him.

In this season of Church history when cells and small groups are a key method of pastoring the Body, *Experiencing the Spirit* could be just the spark needed to start a revival fire in this land! May this book and study guide be the catalyst that causes every denomination to enter into renewal.

Jesus is praying for the Church to move from illumination to demonstration. You hold in your hands the tool you need to begin that journey. May you experience the joy of the divine Helper as you devour this book!

CHUCK D. PIERCE
Director, World Prayer Center

Introduction

THE SURPRISING GRACE
OF THE SPIRIT

Sometimes the Holy Spirit reveals Himself with a surprising kind of mercy. He chose Saul of Tarsus—a proud man, hardened and resistant to God. He waylaid Saul on his mission to Damascus, flashed a bright light in his eyes, knocked him off his horse, struck him blind and—when He finally had Saul's attention—revealed to him the infinite depths of God's love. Paul would later write of this violent encounter, "I was shown mercy because I acted in ignorance...The grace of our Lord was poured out on me abundantly" (1 Tim. 1:13,14).

That's not how most of us think of the Holy Spirit. We've been taught that the Spirit is a "gentleman" who would never do anything you didn't ask Him to do. That only shows how little we understand the grace of God. There are times when God's love for us demands that He move in forceful ways. He may not actually violate our will but, as Saul discovered, when He wants to set our feet on a new path He can be VERY persuasive! Lewis Sperry Chafer, founder of Dallas Theological Seminary, described the grace of God in his salvation, saying, "I kicked, fought against God, and resisted...and God did all the rest."

That's very much the testimony of how I came to experience the Holy Spirit. I wish I could say I diligently sought after God and desired His presence with all my heart, but that's not how it happened. My relationship with the Spirit was, for many years, the story of His wooing and pursuing—and my resisting and rejecting.

NO EXPERIENCE NECESSARY

I grew up in a very conservative, liturgical church where I received much teaching, but little practical understanding, of what it means to live as a Christian. For many in my denomination, Christianity was primarily a matter of faithfully walking through rituals and living a moral life. Personal experience with God was virtually nonexistent. If God had somehow ceased to exist, we would have hardly noticed.

My freshman year in college, I got involved with a well-known campus ministry and committed my life to the Lord. The leaders in this ministry encouraged us to seek the Lord, but were very careful to warn us not to go "too far" and get off course by "seeking experiences." Their attitude was that experiences with God were of questionable validity and should not be sought or emphasized.

Four years of college were followed by two years on staff with this ministry. Again we were taught against seeking experiences—particularly "charismatic" experiences with the Holy Spirit. Even more forceful than the teaching was the obvious fact that those who claimed to have had these experiences were immediately shunned by the rest of the group. When a fellow staff member admitted to having an encounter with the Holy Spirit and speaking in tongues, he was fired! I came to view the Holy Spirit almost as a disease. Those who were infected by Him needed to be quarantined so they didn't contaminate anyone else.

In 1972, I enrolled in Dallas Theological Seminary. Dallas Seminary places a strong emphasis on spiritual maturity, personal integrity and the teaching of the Word, and is widely considered to be among the finest seminaries in the world. It is also a school that takes a strong stand against experiences with the Holy Spirit. Although theological discussion was encouraged on many subjects, it was not considered acceptable to study the charismatic view of

Christianity. In all my classes at Dallas, we were never once assigned to read a book or article expressing a charismatic viewpoint.

Like most Dallas students, I didn't listen to charismatic speakers, attend charismatic conferences or read charismatic books. In fact, I prided myself on only shopping at Christian bookstores that did not carry books by charismatic authors! Having no direct contact with charismatics, all I knew about the Spirit's "charismatic" ministry came from the many books in my library written against it. I was thoroughly convinced that charismatics were not only wrong but dangerous, and I didn't want to "pollute" my mind by listening to anything they had to say.

In 1978, I graduated from Dallas with honors, earning a Th.M. in New Testament Literature and Exegesis. Translated into English, that means I spent four years in a detailed study of the Bible, which included reading the entire New Testament in the original Greek.

While in seminary, I had planted a church in a nearby town. When I graduated, I became its pastor. As pastor, I passed on to my congregation the attitudes I had been taught, regularly warning them against the dangers of seeking experiences.

On one occasion I received a phone call from one of my members. He had seen the car of a well-known charismatic in town parked in front of another member's home and was calling to warn me. I immediately followed up on that call, concerned that the member in question not be led astray by contact with a charismatic!

GOD'S PERSISTENT GRACE

During this time, a curious pattern was emerging. Although intellectually convinced that charismatics were way off base, at a deeper level I was crying out for something more in my walk with the Lord.

From time to time, as I read the New Testament I would feel a profound sense of dissatisfaction with my Christian life. It was clear to me that the people in the Bible experienced a level of relationship with God that I knew very little about.

Every few years God would bring up the issue of the Holy Spirit in a way that left me feeling very uncomfortable. Sometimes it would be through my study of the Word. On one occasion while in seminary I chose to write a paper on the word "healing" in Isaiah 53, intending to disprove the charismatic notion that this referred to physical healing. Applying the principles of biblical exegesis as I was taught, I worked through the passage in Hebrew and did a detailed word study on the key terms. As I studied, however, it became increasingly clear to me that Isaiah 53 *is* referring to physical healing. This left me in an uncomfortable situation. No matter what the text clearly taught, I knew it would not be acceptable at Dallas Theological Seminary to reach this conclusion. Deeply troubled in my spirit, I found a different topic for my paper.

After several incidents like this in my personal study of the Word, I was left with many unanswered questions. I longed to be free to talk with someone about the Holy Spirit, but as spiritual leader of my church, I could not afford to let my questioning be known. If my congregation knew that I was even *considering the possibility* that some of these things could be valid, I would have faced instant rejection.

One Sunday morning I was sitting in church during the worship service, preparing to give my Sunday message. As I listened to the hymns being sung, I again began to ponder the Holy Spirit's ministry, and again I wished there were someone I could dialogue with.

As I sat there thinking, I remembered a couple, Bob and Pat Jarrard, who had visited our church six months earlier. The Jarrards had graduated from a charismatic Bible school, and I thought perhaps I could talk with them about the Holy Spirit. But I hadn't seen them for six months. Without even thinking, I prayed a silent prayer. *Lord, if all this is real, let the Jarrards come back and attend our church so I can have someone to answer my questions about the Holy Spirit.*

Not more than ten seconds after I prayed, the door of the church opened and the entire Jarrard family walked in! I was so shaken that I pushed the entire issue out of my mind. I never did ask them any of my questions.

Although the Jarrards did not remain in our church long, during the next few years we developed a curious friendship with Bob and Pat.

Every morning Pat Jarrard would begin her day by spending several hours with the Lord. During that time God would "put on her heart" the people she was to pray for that day. For the next five years, every time someone in our family was sick, God would put us on Pat's heart.

We might not hear from Pat for six months, but when someone in the family got sick, Pat would call. She'd usually say something like, "Hi! This is Pat. The Lord put you guys on my heart today and I wondered, is there anything I can pray for?"

Pat would usually come by and pray for whoever was sick, and sometimes she would even pray in tongues. Invariably, our sick family member would be completely healed within hours! This didn't just happen once or twice. It probably happened thirty times in a five-year period! This got to be a joke with our kids. When someone got sick they'd say, "I guess it's time for Pat to call!" And she always would!

This made me very uncomfortable. On Sundays I would teach that healing and speaking in tongues were not for today, yet time and again this charismatic woman would come to my house, pray for my family and they would be healed!

During the course of these years—through my own study of the Word and through the experience of God's healing power in our own family—most of my intellectual objections to the Spirit's charismatic ministries gradually evaporated. I came to the point that I could admit that many of the arguments I had been taught against the Spirit's ministry were not valid. I could admit that maybe God *does* still give the gift of healing, and if He does, Pat Jarrard probably had it. I could even admit that perhaps, on rare occasions, He may even give some people the gift of tongues.

There was, however, one thing of which I was still absolutely certain: Even if some of the charismatic gifts were valid today, *they were not for everyone and they* certainly *weren't for me!* I didn't want those things in my life, and I didn't want them in my church. I knew the price I would have to pay to embrace those things, and I was not willing to pay it.

I continued to teach very strongly against the experiential manifestations of the Holy Spirit.

THE SEVERITY OF GOD'S GRACE

In the fall of 1982, the Spirit of God poured into my life the same kind of abundant grace He had shown the apostle Paul.

In His infinite love and wisdom, God removed His hand of protection and allowed the enemy to put me through a year that can only be described as a year from hell! In the months to follow I experienced what was certainly the worst year of my life.

It began with a kidney stone that put me in the hospital for a week, and continued with a rapid succession of illnesses, including strep throat, pneumonia and a case of bronchitis that lasted for weeks. For months that winter I was so sick that I would get up to preach on Sunday morning, return home and go back to bed until the following Sunday.

With a sick, virtually absentee pastor at the helm, my church began to flounder. I was simply unable physically to do the kind of day-to-day work necessary to keep a church healthy.

During that time, my three children were also continually

sick. Not a week went by that we didn't take at least one family member to visit the doctor. We frequently scheduled multiple appointments. My wife, Linda, kept a schedule on the refrigerator to track "who got which medicine when."

Throughout our physical trials, Pat Jarrard never called. In our desperation, we called her and *asked* her to pray, but no healing resulted. When we asked why we weren't being healed by her prayers this time, Pat replied, "Maybe God wants to teach you to pray for healing yourself." That did *not* encourage us!

When spring finally arrived and we thought things might begin to improve, all three children came down with chicken pox—one right after the other.

As a result of mounting medical bills, our finances were devastated and we went deeply into debt. I fell into a deep depression that was almost tangible, hanging like a cloud over everything I did.

After six months of continual illness, financial disaster, a struggling church and persistent spiritual oppression, my wife and I were so emotionally drained that we had just about given up on God. I rarely prayed anymore, and I only read the Bible for professional purposes to prepare sermons and Bible studies. On a scale of one to ten, my level of faith and fellowship with God was about minus five.

I felt God had betrayed me. From the time I committed my life to Jesus, I had tried to follow the Lord and serve Him. I knew the Bible inside and out. I had witnessed to hundreds of people and seen many of them come to the Lord. Yet my life was falling apart, and my prayers went unanswered. This was not the abundant Christian life Jesus had promised His followers! In my bitterness, I was making serious plans to drop out of the pastorate, move back to Florida and take up a secular job.

One day near the end of that year, early in October 1983, I was sitting with a friend in a small café where we met weekly to discuss the problems of the world and ponder great theological issues. On this particular day, we were commiserating over the dryness of our Christian experience and questioning why the Christian life just didn't seem to "work."

At one point my friend stopped, looked me right in the eye and said, "I don't claim to know how this all is supposed to work, but I think it has something to do with the Holy Spirit!"

I knew he was right. I didn't understand it, but I knew the answer had something to do with the Holy Spirit. Yet, in spite of my misery, I was unwilling to call out to Him for help.

THE VOICE OF GOD

The following Monday afternoon I was sitting at my desk beginning my preparations for the next Sunday's message. By this point, message preparation was not a matter of prayer and inspiration, but a mechanical process of study and application. My heart was no longer in the ministry. I was simply biding my time until things came together for us to leave the church and move back to our family home in Florida.

As I sat there at my desk that day, the unexpected happened: God spoke to me. This was not an audible voice, but it spoke clearly and powerfully into my spirit. There could be no doubt it was God.

He asked me two questions. First He asked, "If the church would never grow, would you still love Me?"

I had to stop and think about that. The primary root of my depression was the fact that the church I had founded and poured my life into for ten years was now floundering badly. As I pondered God's question, I remembered the close times I had enjoyed with the Lord over the years and suddenly realized that, in spite of all that had happened, I really did love Him! I answered, "Yes, Lord, even if I never see this church grow, I'll still love You."

He then asked, "If you never move to Florida, would you still love Me?" Again I struggled. For months Linda and I had set our hopes on moving back to Florida. That's where our friends and family were. When everything else seemed hopeless, we would dream of returning to Florida. We believed that *somehow* everything would be better once we were there.

I finally recognized that I must submit my hopes to Him in this area also. I answered, "Yes, Lord. Even if I never move back to Florida, I'll still love You!"

He then spoke one more phrase: "Seek first My kingdom and My righteousness."

I immediately got out an index card and wrote down His instruction, which I kept on my desk for years afterward. I wasn't nearly so impressed by what God said as I was by the fact that *I knew God had spoken!* All my life I had been taught that God doesn't speak to people anymore. But God *had* spoken to me! I was still depressed, but I knew God had *spoken.*

A SURPRISING VISITATION

A week later, Steve Mathers, a friend of ours from Minneapolis, was in town on business. Although Steve was a charismatic, he had never tried to push his views on us, and we counted him as one of our closest friends.

As we sat in our living room that Monday evening, Linda and I began to share with Steve what we had experienced in the past year. We told him how we felt God had let us down. We poured out our bitterness over the continual sickness, our frustrations in the church, our financial distress and the unanswered prayers. We described the almost tangible cloud of depression that continually hung over us. Our friend listened intently to the whole story.

Steve didn't patronize us or try to write off our problems with quick, simplistic answers filled with Christian jargon. He didn't say, "You just need to be baptized in the Holy Spirit!" We could see he was genuinely grieved for us. He finally said, "I don't know why God would let you go through all of that, but I know He would not have allowed it to happen if He didn't have a purpose for it. *Just don't give up on God.*"

As the evening drew to a close, Steve asked if he could pray for us. We didn't expect it would do any good, but we let him pray. I don't even remember what Steve prayed, but when he finished praying, he had a vision. We didn't believe in visions, but he had one anyway—right there in our living room! He said, "I'm seeing a picture. I see that you're looking at everything through a stained-glass window, and you can't see clearly, but God's going to do something, and you will."

We didn't understand what that meant and were not at all encouraged by it. By this time we had tried so many ways to find relief, we had become deeply cynical. We went to bed that night as hopeless, as discouraged and as bitter as we had ever been.

When Linda and I woke up the next morning, however, the whole world had *changed.* The depression and bitterness were gone! From the moment we awoke, joyful songs of praise flooded our minds. The Spirit of God had invaded our home and, overnight, we had fallen madly and passionately in love with Jesus! The presence of God was so tangible in our home that we found ourselves in a continual conversation with Him. Our circumstances and the world around us had receded into the background; His presence was now our true reality. We were filled with a hunger for His Word we had not experienced in years. When we opened the Bible and began to read, *He* would speak directly to our hearts!

As days went by, this didn't stop; it only increased. We were consciously experiencing God. We had no idea what had happened. We had no label to describe it. We just knew it was GOD, and it was *wonderful!*

God had mercifully granted us instantaneous deliverance from spiritual oppression. It was the filling, or baptism, of His

Spirit. He had released His river of living water into the dryness of our souls. But God wasn't finished.

Two days after God had first descended upon our home, my wife, Linda, was standing at the kitchen sink washing dishes. The presence of God was there, and she was singing songs of praise to Him. Suddenly she felt something bubbling up deep within her and she knew immediately what it was. She said to herself, almost in horror, *I'm about to speak in tongues!* Fearful that someone might come in and see her, Linda ran to our bedroom and locked the door, then into our bathroom and locked the door, and there in the bathroom, my godly, evangelical wife prayed in tongues for the first time!

I didn't know this had happened, but later that same day I was walking down the hallway in our home, enjoying the presence of God, singing songs of praise to Jesus and feeling overwhelmed with my love for Him. As I sought to express to Him what I was feeling, God spoke to me again. He said simply, "You can pray in tongues if you want to!" Without a moment's hesitation, tongues of praise began to flow from my mouth.

My wife and I had both been taught against tongues for so long, it was difficult for us to talk about what had happened. We didn't tell each other for more than a week!

As Linda and I finally sat down to talk about what had happened to us, we knew we had crossed a line into unknown territory. We had received much teaching *against* spiritual experiences, but had never been taught much *about* experiencing the Spirit. We decided to devote an entire year of study through the Bible to see what it taught about experiencing the Holy Spirit. It was a year of incredible discovery. This book is the outgrowth of the things God began to teach us that year.

1

WHO IS THIS HOLY SPIRIT?

Those who regularly drove down Lattimore Street knew the pathetic sight of the old man all too well. His "home" was a jumble of cardboard cartons and trash stashed under the I-35 overpass. His transportation was a rusty grocery cart borrowed from a local market, with a right front wheel that wobbled as he coaxed it along the litter-strewn gutters.

During the summer, he would panhandle under the hot Texas sun for loose change from drivers stopped at the red light at Industrial Boulevard. In the winter, it was easier to root through the filthy dumpsters behind the hotel for scraps of food.

One bitter winter day, he didn't make his usual rounds. At first no one noticed. Even if they had, it was far too miserable a day to brave the sleet and cold of a "blue norther" to go looking for a lonely old man.

Two days later, someone found him. His frail body, wasted away by pneumonia, lay cold and dead in his cardboard "home," surrounded by the crumpled newspapers he had burrowed into in a futile attempt to keep warm.

When the county coroner did the autopsy, he was puzzled to find a safe-deposit box key tightly clasped in the old man's right hand. At first he supposed the old man had just found it on the street, or perhaps even stolen it. An investigation revealed, however, that the deposit box had been issued in the old man's name many years earlier.

What the lawyers found in the box when they opened it two weeks later made a front page article in the city newspaper.

In the box they found the deed to the old man's mansion in Florida, now unoccupied for many years. There were stocks and bonds from an investment portfolio, untouched for more than a decade. They found his diploma from Harvard, a Rolex watch, stacks of crisp $100 bills, small plastic containers filled with gold coins and a diamond ring valued at several thousand dollars.

The old man who had lived in such misery and squalor was, in reality, a very wealthy man. He possessed incredible resources, but had not made use of the resources he possessed.

MAKING THE CHRISTIAN LIFE "WORK"

That old man is a picture of much of the Church today. God has blessed every Christian with incredible resources. He has made us to be kings and priests (see Rev. 1:6, NKJV). He has given us every spiritual blessing (see Eph. 1:3), even granting us authority over all the forces of the enemy (see Luke 10:19). He has made His own omnipotent power available to us (see Eph. 1:19,20).

The Bible is a guide to these resources—and how God intends for us to use them. In John 14:12, Jesus promised that if we believe in Him, we can do not only the same works that He did, but even greater ones. That's power! In his letter to the Ephesians, Paul indicates that the power available to us is like the awesome power displayed at the resurrection of Jesus from the dead (see Eph. 1:19,20). This power will enable us to take the gospel message into all the world (see Acts 1:8), to see people delivered out of darkness into the kingdom of God.

Most Christians, however, have little understanding of the incredible resources God has given us. Many of us instead live in spiritual poverty, living not as supernatural beings who are "partakers of the divine nature" (2 Pet. 1:4, *NKJV*), but living as "mere men" (1 Cor. 3:3).

Christians live from week to week, attending church services, holding Bible studies, going through the rituals we have been told are important to an effective Christian life. But all too often, it's just a religious game. We don't see the kind of results the New Testament Christians witnessed. We barely have enough power to sustain ourselves through the trials and pressures of daily life, much less reach a hurting world.

Yet the key to the supernatural resources of God is in your hand right now! That key is found in the person of the Holy Spirit.

THE IMPORTANCE OF THE HOLY SPIRIT

It's surprising how little the average Christian knows about the Spirit of God. Most Christians can tell you something about the life of Jesus, and most can give you a pretty good idea who God the Father is; but when it comes to the Holy Spirit, they're at a loss for words.

Yet the Bible has a great deal to say about the Holy Spirit. In the first chapter of Genesis, we see Him brooding over the face of the deep, imparting His power and preparing the earth so that life could burst forth at a word from the Creator (see Gen. 1:2). In the last chapter of the Bible, we see the Spirit of God joining with the Bride to intercede for the second coming of Jesus (see Rev. 22:17). Throughout the Word, the Holy Spirit plays a vital part in the work of God on earth.

Why are so many Christians unsure about the Holy Spirit? Some Christians have been taught that it's not right to emphasize the Spirit. They will say, "I don't want to talk about the Holy Spirit. I just want to talk about Jesus." That sounds spiritual, but it is not biblical.

Jesus openly announced that one of the goals of His ministry was to bring people into a dynamic, life-giving relationship with the Spirit of God. He promised, "He who believes in Me, as the Scripture said, 'From his innermost being shall flow rivers of living water.'" (John 7:38, *NASB*). The passage goes on to explain that these rivers of living water are a reference to the ministry of the Holy Spirit (v. 39).

John the Baptist foretold of Jesus, saying, "He will baptize you with the Holy Spirit and with fire" (Luke 3:16). The Holy Spirit was also prominent in the message of the apostles. On the day of Pentecost, Peter proclaimed to thousands that those who believed in Jesus would receive the gift of the Holy Spirit! (See Acts 2:38.)

The writers of the New Testament never hesitated to honor and exalt the Third Person of the Trinity, and they repeatedly stressed the vital importance of living in relationship with Him. On one occasion, Jesus assured the disciples that it was to their advantage for Him to leave and return to heaven so that He could send them the Holy Spirit (see John 16:7). That's an incredible tribute to the importance of the Spirit's ministry! Jesus was saying that it is better to have the Holy Spirit with you than to have the Son of God personally present!

Though the apostles had been with Jesus daily for three years, listening to His teaching, and learning from His example, it wasn't enough. Jesus told his friends that they were not ready to serve Him until they had received the power of the Holy Spirit (see Luke 24:49). If the Holy Spirit was that important to Jesus and the apostles, He should be important to us as well.

I don't believe there is a more crucial truth for Christians today than the truth about the Holy Spirit. Listen to the way great men of God, both evangelical and charismatic, have described the importance of the Spirit's ministry. Jack Hayford, senior pastor of The Church On The Way in Van Nuys,

California, represents a Charismatic view of the Spirit. He describes the importance of the Spirit's work this way:

> It is the Spirit who keeps the Word alive, and progressively being "incarnated" in me...
>
> It is the Spirit who infuses prayer and praise with passion and begets vital faith for the supernatural.
>
> It is the Spirit who teaches and instructs me so that the "mirror" of the Word shines Jesus in and crowds sin out;
>
> It is the Spirit who brings gifts and giftedness for power-ministry to my life...and
>
> It is the Spirit who will bring love, graciousness, and a spirit of unity to my heart; so that I not only love the lost and want to see people brought to Christ, but I love all other Christians, and refuse to become an instrument of injury to Christ's body—the Church.[1]

On the other side of the spectrum we find Bill Bright, president of Campus Crusade for Christ and a leading evangelical speaker. He writes of the Spirit's ministry this way:

> He guides us (John 16:13), empowers us (Mic. 3:8) and makes us holy (Rom. 15:16). He bears witness in our lives (Rom. 8:16), comforts us (John 14:16-26), gives us joy (Rom. 14:17)...
>
> As our teacher of spiritual truths, the Holy Spirit illuminates our minds with insights into the mind of Christ (1 Cor. 2:12,13) and reveals to us the hidden things of God (Isa. 40:13,14)...
>
> As you are filled with the Holy Spirit, the Bible becomes alive, prayer becomes vital, your witness becomes effective and obedience becomes a joy. Then, as a result of your obedience in these areas, your faith grows and you become more mature in your spiritual life.[2]

No matter where they are on the theological spectrum, godly men and women agree that the Holy Spirit is the key to the Christian life. I believe it's safe to say that

No matter how much you know about the Bible,
No matter how much you discipline yourself,
No matter how hard you try to serve and please God,

if you are not properly related to the Spirit of God, the Christian life will not work for you. That's because the Christian life is not a ritual or a set of teachings but a relationship—a relationship with God through His Holy Spirit.

The Holy Spirit was given to make the Christian life *experiential*—to make Jesus real, not only in your understanding but also in your life.

The purpose of this book is to help you to enter into that vital relationship with the Holy Spirit so you can experience, in a greater way, the resources of God.

Real Life Testimony

Jeff and Julie sat on opposite ends of the couch in the pastor's office. From the bitterness and anger evident on their faces, Pastor Bill Johnson suspected the couple had argued all the way to the counseling appointment.

Pastor Johnson recognized almost from the start that Jeff and Julie had problems in their relationship, but he had not suspected things would get this bad so quickly. They had only been married for six months and already the love and romance that had drawn them together had worn so thin that both were talking divorce.

As Jeff and Julie began to pour their hearts out, an all-too-familiar pattern emerged. Jeff harbored a growing bitterness toward Julie because she wasn't "meeting his needs." He felt cheated and, in his anger, tried to demand the things she wouldn't willingly give. Julie, on the other hand, felt "used" rather than "loved," and as a result she could hardly stand to be with Jeff.

Guessing as to the underlying problem, Pastor Johnson began to lovingly probe their relationship with some penetrating questions. He particularly focused on Jeff, asking him about his parents' marriage and about his dating relationships.

After listening carefully to everything Jeff said, Pastor Johnson was silent for a few moments. Finally he said, "Jeff, I hope I don't offend you by saying this, but I believe your problem is that you've never learned to relate to a woman as a person. You've always seen women as objects to meet your needs. The result is that you can't really love Julie; you just use her to meet your needs. And Julie can't relate to you as a person and give you the love she wants to give you, because you don't see her as a person."

As Pastor Johnson spoke, Jeff was pierced to the heart. Incident after incident flashed across his mind. In a moment of God-given insight, he saw his problem. Tears welled in his eyes and he looked over at Julie, seeing for the first time the wounding he had caused. From quivering lips he said, "Oh Julie! I'm sorry I've hurt you so!"

By the grace of God, Jeff learned to relate to Julie. And in the months that followed, their love began to grow and deepen.

RELATING TO THE SPIRIT

On a human level, we can't have a relationship with someone unless we are able to see that individual as a person—a person with his or her own interests, concerns, needs and desires. In a very real sense, the same thing is true of a relationship with the Holy Spirit.

Many Christians have a difficult time relating to the Holy Spirit because they don't understand who He is. They tend to think of the Holy Spirit as an impersonal "higher power" like the mysterious Force in *Star Wars*. Others think of Him only as a source of power and blessing. They just want to "plug in" and receive what they need. Still others think of the Holy Spirit as an influence for good, similar to the conscience.

But you can't have a relationship with a force or an influence or even a power source. You might manipulate a force, plug in to a power supply or respond to an influence, but you can never have a love relationship with anything less than a person.

THE SPIRIT IS A PERSON

What do we mean when we say that the Holy Spirit is a person? We certainly don't mean that He is a being with a physical body. Having a physical body is not what makes you a person. When you die and your spirit leaves your body, you will still be a person.

Don Stewart, in his book *95 Questions People Ask About the Holy Spirit*, describes the "personhood" of the Spirit. "By 'person' we mean one who has his own identity or individuality as a rational being."[3] Stewart goes on to describe four ways the Spirit can be observed to be a person:

First of all, the Holy Spirit *has the characteristics of a person.* He is a thinking being. He has intellect (see 1 Cor. 2:10,11). He is an emotional being with a full range of emotions (see Rom. 15:30; Heb. 10:29). He is a choosing being with a will to choose and to make decisions (1 Cor. 12:11).

Second, the Holy Spirit *acts like a person.* He does things only a person can do—He teaches (see John 14:26), He speaks (see Gal. 4:6), He comforts (see John 16:7), He prays (see Rom. 8:26).

Third, the Holy Spirit *is treated like a person*. He can be lied to (see Acts 5:3). He can be grieved (see Eph. 4:30). He can be disobeyed (see Acts 7:51). Stewart writes, "Whenever we find the Holy Spirit in a historical narrative, He is consistently treated as though He is a person, never as anything less."[4]

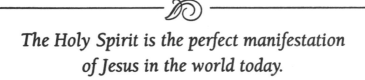

The Holy Spirit is the perfect manifestation of Jesus in the world today.

Finally, the Holy Spirit *is part of the Trinity*. He is identified as an equal with the other Persons in the trinity (see Matt. 28:19; 2 Cor. 13:14). He shares with Jesus and the Father the mysterious relationship that eternally exists within the Godhead.

Jesus described the kind of relationship that exists within the Trinity with statements like "I and the Father are one" (John 10:30), "Anyone who has seen me has seen the Father" (John 14:9) and "He who rejects me rejects him who sent me" (Luke 10:16).

That same kind of unity exists between Jesus and the Spirit. Just as Jesus was sent by the Father to be the visible manifestation of the invisible God, so the Holy Spirit was sent by Jesus to perfectly manifest His presence in the lives of His people. Just as those who received Jesus also received the Father, so those who receive the Spirit receive Jesus.

The Holy Spirit is the perfect manifestation of Jesus in the world today. That's why it does not detract from Jesus to talk about the Holy Spirit. The one who relates to the Spirit is relating to Jesus, so the more you develop your relationship with the Holy Spirit, the closer your walk with Jesus will be.

Some have taught that it's not right to give praise to the Holy Spirit, saying that the Spirit should never be prayed to or worshiped. I don't see that prohibition in the Bible. If the Spirit is God, then it is proper to worship Him. If worship is the act of honoring or attributing worth to God, then the Spirit is just as much worthy of worship as the Father and Son, for He is fully equal to the Father and Son in His deity and personhood.

The writers of the Bible never hesitate to give praise and honor to the Holy Spirit. They repeatedly recount His deeds and exalt His attributes. The very act of calling Him the *Holy* Spirit is an act of praise acknowledging the holiness of His character (see Ps. 139:7).

Although not the norm, prayer to the Spirit is not without biblical precedent, and nowhere is it prohibited. God instructed Ezekiel to prophesy to the breath (Spirit) and call on the Spirit of God to "come from the four winds" and "breathe into these slain, that they may live" (Ezek. 37:9,10). From its earliest days, the Church has prayed prayers of invocation to the Holy Spirit, asking Him to perform His work. Even today, if you look at the hymnals of almost any denomination, you will find hymns addressed to the Spirit, calling on Him to come and minister to His people.

KNOWING THE SPIRIT

If the Spirit is a person, how do we relate to Him? What does it mean to know a person we cannot see?

First and foremost, a relationship between any two people involves mutual interaction. They communicate with each other. They *experience* each other.

I have a relationship with my wife. We talk to each other. I share my heart with her, and she shares her heart with me. I can experience her presence. We can hold hands. We can embrace. I do things to please her, and she does things to please me. We express our love to each other. There is two-way interaction. That's what relationship is all about.

Let's suppose I decide to have a relationship with Abraham Lincoln. I might study Lincoln's life to learn what he was like. I could read his writings and the writings of those who knew him. I could gain a great appreciation for the kind of person he was and the things he accomplished. I could even travel to Lincoln's tomb, stand near where his body lies and attempt to talk to him. But I would not have entered into a relationship with Honest Abe.

Relationship requires interaction. Abe could never talk to me, acknowledge my presence, shake my hand or give me a pat on the back. Without the ability to experience Lincoln, I can never have a true relationship with him. I may end up knowing *about* him, but I can never *know* him.

There is great debate today in the Church over the issue of experiencing the Holy Spirit. Some teach that God said all He had to say to us by the end of the first century, that He has cut off all communication with His people. They believe the Christian life to be nonexperiential, a matter of learning about God from the Bible and trying to do what would please Him. They teach that we can talk to God in prayer and read what He said to others in the past, but that we cannot experience Him ourselves. If that is true, we are in a sad condition, for we can have no more relationship with God than we can with Abe Lincoln.

However, the Bible presents us with a different view of the Christian life. The Bible is our instruction manual for the Christian life, written to teach us how to live in relationship with God. The people given in the Bible as examples of how to walk with God were people who actually experienced God. They didn't just know *about* God; they interacted with Him.

They sensed when the Holy Spirit's power was manifested

(see 1 Cor. 5:4). They recognized His hand in the working of healings and miracles (see Acts, 1 Cor. 12). They heard His voice and were confident in their ability to ask questions and receive answers from Him (see Gen. 25:22,23; Dan. 2:16-19). They were led by the Spirit, and they allowed His leadings to direct their actions (see Acts 16:7). Their lives involved constant two-way communication with the Spirit of God.

In fact, the only model the Bible gives us for walking with God is an experiential model. Much of the Bible is a record of experiences with God. The Word describes men and women who placed great importance on spiritual experiences and often made crucial decisions on the basis of those experiences (see Matt. 1:20; 2:13). One of the most important theological decisions in the history of the Church—the inclusion of Gentiles in the Church—was made on the basis of a spiritual experience, when the Holy Spirit fell on a group of Gentiles, causing them to speak in tongues (see Acts 15:7,8,19).

EXPERIENCING THE HOLY SPIRIT

The tendency of today's evangelical church to reject spiritual experiences is a relatively recent development. In the late nineteenth century, D. L. Moody, one of the greatest evangelical leaders of his day, attributed the success of his ministry to a dramatic spiritual experience he called his "baptism of the Holy Spirit."

Moody wrote that he had been crying out to God for the power of the Spirit. In response to his persistent prayer the Holy Spirit fell upon him:

> One day, in the city of New York—oh, what a day! I cannot describe it, I seldom refer to it; it is almost too sacred an experience to name. I can only say that God revealed Himself to me, and I had such an experience of His love

that I had to ask Him to stay His hand. I went to preaching again. The sermons were not different; I did not present any new truths, and yet hundreds were converted. I would not now be placed back where I was before that blessed experience if you should give me all the world.[5]

It was common in Moody's day for evangelical leaders to urge their followers to seek a deeper experience with the Spirit. Another early evangelical leader, Adoniram Judson Gordon, held healing services in his church, resulting in many testimonies of miraculous healings.

Merill Unger, professor of Old Testament Studies at Dallas Theological Seminary from 1948 to 1967 and the editor of *Unger's Bible Dictionary*, also believed in divine healing. He expressed his views on the spiritual gift of healing this way:

Such endowments of the Holy Spirit...were meant to continue in use throughout the Church age and to be in use today....When rightly used, gifts of healing produce one of life's greatest blessings. Healing of the believer's body is divinely designed to crown confession of sin and honor the life dedicated to the Lord....The Lord waits to touch the weak bodies of His redeemed ones and quicken them to fulfill all His purpose for them in this life.[6]

Lewis Sperry Chafer, founder of Dallas Theological Seminary, described how following subjective "leadings" of the Spirit brought him success in evangelism.

Charles Spurgeon, the great Baptist preacher, eagerly anticipated the later turn-of-the-century Pentecostal outpouring and its release of prophetic giftings when he wrote in 1855:

Another great work of the Holy Spirit which is not accomplished is the bringing on of the latter-day glory. In a few more years—I know not when, I know not how—the Holy Spirit will be poured out in far different style from the present. My eyes flash with the thought that very likely I shall live to see the outpouring of the Spirit; when "the sons and the daughters of God shall prophesy, and the young men shall see visions, and the old men shall dream dreams."[7]

While none of these men were charismatic or Pentecostal, they strongly believed that the experience of the Spirit was a vital element in the Christian life.

I believe it is time for all of the Church—whether evangelical, charismatic, Pentecostal or "Third Wave"—to take a fresh look at the ministry of the Holy Spirit, so that together we can press on into all the Spirit has to offer.

It's time for the Church to lay down its carefully crafted doctrinal positions and allow God to restore us to a truly biblical Christianity, in which God is not only studied and obeyed, but experienced.

2

THE INDWELLING SPIRIT: WHY THE HOLY SPIRIT WANTS TO LIVE IN YOU!

A fable from the land of India is often told of four blind men who heard of a wondrous animal called an elephant. Determined to learn more about this strange creature, they arranged to go and "see" it for themselves.

Entering the compound where the elephant was kept, the blind men groped forward until they encountered the beast. The first man bumped against the elephant's side. He carefully ran his hands up and down, then back and forth along the dusty hide of the mammoth animal, then loudly announced to his friends, "I see what an elephant is like! An elephant is like a wall!"

The second blind man encountered the elephant's leg. Grasping the leg in his trembling hands, he answered back, "What are you talking about! An elephant is not at all like a wall. An elephant is like a tree!"

Meanwhile, the third blind man ran into the elephant's tusk. Feeling its hard, sharply pointed tip, he rebuked his friends. "What foolishness is this? You are both insane! An elephant is nothing like a wall or a tree. I can tell very plainly that an elephant is like a spear!"

The fourth blind man encountered the elephant's powerful, coiling trunk. Leaping back from it in terror, he exclaimed, "You are all wrong! For I know for a fact that an elephant is like a giant snake!"

The blind men left the compound in a heated argument about the true nature of an elephant. Each was thoroughly convinced that he was right and the others wrong. Each based his judgment on his own personal experience, never suspecting that there was far more to an elephant than what any one of them could comprehend.

THE DIVERSITY OF THE SPIRIT'S WORK

The Bible uses many different terms to describe the ministries of the Holy Spirit. His various works include convicting of sin, regenerating, hovering, coming upon, sealing, filling, baptizing, speaking, leading, indwelling, teaching and many more!

For most of us, different activities bring out different sides of our personalities. Around the church office, my wife appears to be quiet, thoughtful and efficient. If you knew her only in her "office" mode, you might be shocked to see her antics at the ballpark. When Linda passes through the gates of a baseball stadium, her quiet demeanor gets lost in the crowd and a different side of her personality emerges. Linda becomes a rabid baseball fan! When her team hits a home run, she'll jump up and down, waving her arms and cheering loudly till the batter reaches home plate.

This kind of change is not uncommon for any of us as we move from one activity to another. That's why it's good for a couple contemplating marriage to spend time together in a lot of different situations. You can't really *know* someone until you've seen that person in a variety of situations.

The same is true of the Holy Spirit. Different activities of the Spirit reveal different aspects of His personality. If you've only known the Spirit when He convicts you of sin (see John 16:9), you may be surprised when you see Him releasing power to heal (see Acts 5:16). You can experience Him as He gives prophetic words (see 1 Cor. 12:10), but still not recognize Him in His role as sanctifier (see 1 Thess. 5:23). You won't really know who the Spirit is until you have seen Him in the diversity of His ministries.

To better understand the Spirit and His ministries, it may be helpful to examine His work under two broad categories—His *indwelling* ministry and His *empowering* ministry.

THE INDWELLING AND EMPOWERING SPIRIT

Many passages in the Bible describe the Holy Spirit living within the hearts of His people. These passages portray the *indwelling* Spirit as the source of a sanctifying work which enables Christians to live holier lives (see Ezek. 36:27; Rom. 8:9-13; 1 Cor. 6:19,20). These passages don't make reference to supernatural manifestations. There is no release of charismatic gifts, prophetic utterances or miraculous power. These passages describe a quiet work of the Spirit, focusing on the importance of obedience, repentance and spiritual growth.

In a different set of passages the Holy Spirit is described not as living *within* His people, but as *coming upon*, *falling upon*, or being *poured out upon* them. These passages describe an *empowering* work that equips God's people to minister. This empowering ministry reveals a completely different side of the Spirit's personality. When the Spirit comes upon His people miracles take place. Spiritual gifts are imparted. Prophecies are given. (See Num. 24:2,3; 1 Sam. 10:10; 19:20-23; Joel 2:28; Acts 19:6.)

The indwelling and empowering ministries of the Holy Spirit have entirely different purposes and operate in very different ways, but it is God's will for the Spirit to perform both of these in your life. You may find it helpful to think of these ministries like this:

The Spirit's *indwelling* is designed to *mature* us, causing us to grow in the Lord.

The Spirit's *empowering* is designed to *equip* us, enabling us to serve the Lord.

To put it another way:

The Spirit *indwells* us to give us victory over sin, making us *holy*.

The Spirit *empowers* us to give us *tools for ministry*, making us *effective*.

Or:

The Spirit *lives within you* to give you the *character of Christ.*

The Spirit *comes upon you* in power to give you the *ministry of Christ.*

Both of these ministries are *essential* if we are to reach our full potential in Christ. The New Testament teaches that the Holy Spirit is God's provision for Christian living. Until we embrace the fullness of the Spirit's ministry we will always be lacking. If we are to fulfill God's purposes and accomplish the destiny for which He created us, we need to receive *all* that the Spirit was sent to provide.

All too often, however, as we set out to understand the work of the Spirit, we come with the attitude of the blind Indians. We come to the Holy Spirit from different directions, gain some knowledge about Him and quickly form wildly diverse opinions about what the Spirit of God is—and is not—like. And what He will—and will not—do.

Most evangelicals tend to focus on the Spirit's indwelling ministry. They teach that the job of the Spirit is to work quietly within you, in an unemotional and nonexperiential way, to build you toward maturity in the Lord. It's easy for a Christian growing up in an evangelical environment to assume that's all the Holy Spirit does. Any other work attributed to the Spirit is therefore suspect.

Christians in the Pentecostal and charismatic movements tend to focus on the empowering work of the Spirit. Healings and prophetic words are common occurrences in many of these churches. In such an environment, it's easy to assume that the Holy Spirit is interested only in demonstrations of power. Some in these movements may even question whether a Christian who is not operating in supernatural power has the Holy Spirit within him.

The result is that the Church is divided into opposing factions. Like the Indian blind men, these factions devote much energy and effort proving their assumptions about what the Holy Spirit is really like.

In reality, the work of the Holy Spirit includes both of these ministries—and much more. No matter which perspective we come from, the starting point for growth is to put away our defensiveness and humbly admit there is more to the Holy Spirit than what any of us have personally encountered. Let's begin by looking at the Spirit's *indwelling* ministry.

THE INDWELLING SPIRIT

The great evangelist H. A. Ironside was preaching on a busy street corner in a Northeastern city when a well-dressed man walked up and began to ridicule and jeer. Ironside recognized the heckler as a university professor and a well-known and vocal atheist. This professor was full of bitterness and anger against all religion, but especially against Christianity.

As Ironside tried to continue his message, the man began to shout objections. He criticized the Bible and labeled Christians as ignorant fools. He loudly proclaimed, "There is no God! Jesus is a myth!"

At first, Ironside tried to ignore the man, but the professor grew more and more belligerent, taunting Ironside to respond to his intellectual arguments. Finally the man shouted, "I challenge you to a debate! Are you afraid to debate me?"

Ironside knew that an intellectual debate with this man would accomplish nothing, but he also knew that he must respond to the man's attack. "I accept your challenge, sir," he shouted, "but on one condition! When you come to the debate, I ask that you bring with you ten men and women whose lives have been changed for the better by the message of atheism!

"Bring some alcoholics and drug addicts who have been set free by atheism's power. Bring former prostitutes and criminals whose lives have been changed, who are now moral and responsible individuals. Bring outcasts who had no hope and have them tell us how becoming atheists has lifted them out of the pit!

"And sir," Ironside concluded, "if you can find ten such men and women, I will be happy to debate you. And when I come, I will gladly bring with me two hundred men and women from this very city whose lives have been transformed in just those ways by the power of the gospel of Jesus Christ!"

As the professor heard Ironside's challenge, he stopped his jeering, turned and walked away without a word. He knew that, for all its pretense, atheism had no power to change lives. JESUS changes lives.

That proud professor could not meet Ironside's challenge. But Ironside's part of the challenge would not have been at all difficult to meet. You can go into any city in this nation and find hundreds of people whose lives have been changed in the way Ironside described.

In my church today, I can point out person after person who has been hopeless, rebellious and immoral; people who were alcoholics and drug addicts; women who have had abortions; men who have been enslaved by pornography; individuals who have been deeply ensnared in witchcraft and the occult; and people who were so full of despair they attempted to take their own lives.

Yet as you look at these people today, they are godly, responsible individuals. They are loving parents with fine families. They are full of hope, and every one of them will tell you that what changed their lives was a relationship with Jesus Christ.

Christ can do what no other religious leader has ever offered to do: He can change lives. And He does it *through the indwelling ministry of the Holy Spirit*. The indwelling Spirit is the Spirit of Jesus living in the hearts of His people, sent to give them new hope, new love, new peace, new joy and new direction.

This ministry is foundational to everything else in the Christian life. Through the indwelling Spirit we are *sealed* in Christ and given an inner assurance that we belong to Him (see 2 Cor. 1:22). Through the indwelling Spirit we experience a fundamental change in our innermost beings. Old habits drop away and old bondages are broken. We find we have become "new creations," being conformed more and more to the character of the Lord Jesus Christ (2 Cor. 5:17).

As Walvoord writes, "The blessed fact that God has made the earthly bodies of Christians His present earthly temple renders to life and service a power and significance which is at the heart of all Christian experience."[1]

I define the Spirit's indwelling ministry this way:

The indwelling ministry of the Holy Spirit is the ministry in which He lives in a believer's heart to produce the character of Jesus in the believer's life.

"BEHOLD, I DO A NEW THING!"

The indwelling of the Holy Spirit is a New Testament ministry. During Old Testament times, the Spirit of God was *with* His people and they enjoyed the fellowship of His presence. He would also come upon certain ones to empower them for specific tasks, but He did not dwell in them on a continuing basis.

As we read the Old Testament Scriptures, we discover that shortly after the destruction of Solomon's Temple, Israel's prophets began to predict a fundamental change in the way God would relate to His people. They prophesied that God would cause His *Ruach Ha Kodesh*, His Holy Spirit, to dwell *within* the hearts of His people. Through Ezekiel, the Lord announced, "I will put my Spirit in you and move you to follow my decrees and be careful to keep my laws" (Ezek. 36:27). God promised His people that His Spirit would take up residence in their hearts to provide a powerful new resource for holy living!

The Old Testament saints must have marveled at that thought! They had known the manifest presence of the Holy Spirit as the *Shekinah* glory, "the dazzling light of God's presence" (2 Chron. 7:1, *TEV*) which resided in the holiest, most sacred part of the Temple. But through Ezekiel, God promised that this *Shekinah* would one day come to dwell in the hearts of mortal human beings!

Jesus repeatedly talked about what this indwelling Spirit would accomplish. At the Feast of the Tabernacles, He described the indwelling Spirit as an artesian well in the believer's heart, from which a river of living water—the very life of God—would flow (see John 7:38). This same passage indicates that this ministry of the Spirit would begin *after Jesus was glorified* (see v. 39).

On the night before His crucifixion, Jesus again repeated Ezekiel's promise. He told His disciples that the Holy Spirit was "with" them but would, in the very near future, be "in" them

(John 14:17). He went on to describe the fruit this change would produce. The indwelling Spirit would lead them into all truth and reveal the things of Jesus to them (see John 14—16).

To the disciples, all of this probably seemed incomprehensible. How could they have understood what He was saying? They certainly had little time to ponder this promise, for within hours of hearing it they saw their Lord betrayed and crucified. All their hopes seemed destroyed. They were consumed by confusion and fear.

Then, on the third day, they began to hear reports of Jesus' resurrection. On the evening of that first Easter Sunday they were huddled together in the upper room, eagerly debating the significance of the reports they had heard. Suddenly, Jesus Himself appeared to them. They could see the nail prints in His hands and the deep wound in His side. This was the same Jesus they had seen crucified, but He was also different. He was no longer limited by physical restraints. He could pass through locked doors and travel from place to place instantaneously. *He was now in a glorified body* (see John 20:19).

He breathed on them and said, "Receive the Holy Spirit" (John 20:22). This is a highly significant verse. As God breathed the "breath" of physical life into Adam in Genesis 2, Jesus now imparts the very "breath" of God, the Holy Spirit, into His loyal followers.

There is great debate in some circles about what happened at that point. When Jesus imparted the Spirit to them, what did they receive? Some have found in this passage a contradiction to the events recorded in Acts, chapter 2. Is this John's version of the Pentecost story? No, there is no contradiction here. What the Spirit accomplishes in John 20 is very different from what He does in Acts 2.

This was not the release of the Holy Spirit's power. That did not take place until the day of Pentecost. This was an altogether different work of the Spirit. I believe the glorified Christ appeared to them here to fulfill His promise of John 7:39 and 14:17. He came to implant within them the river of living water, to impart the *indwelling* Spirit of God.

What took place that Sunday evening was the initiation of the Holy Spirit's indwelling ministry. When Jesus breathed on them and said, "Receive the Holy Spirit," I believe they received Him! The Spirit of God entered into their physical bodies and took up residence in them.

That event marked a major transition in God's way of dealing with His people. From that moment on, the Spirit of God has dwelt in His people. Because of this, we have resources that the Old Testament saints never had.

WHY THE SPIRIT WANTS TO LIVE IN YOU

Why would the Spirit of God want to live inside people like you and me? He lives in our hearts to enable us to live life on a new level. He is working to *change* us from the inside out, so that we may become more and more like Jesus.

On Mount Sinai, God's people were given an *external* law that defined holiness. The Law was righteous and good, but it lacked power. The Law couldn't give men and women the power to live holy lives.

In Jeremiah 31:33, however, God promised that He would one day write His law on the hearts of His people. And that is what the indwelling of the Holy Spirit accomplishes, placing God's holiness *within* you. That's why your life changed the moment you came to know Jesus. That's why people share testimonies of how knowing Jesus has transformed their lives and saved their marriages. When the Holy Spirit comes to live within you, He *changes* you!

Some years ago, a young man named Shane moved to our town from a large city in the northeast United States. Shane came from a gang-infested inner-city neighborhood. Drugs, sexual immorality and crime were all he had known from his earliest memories. He had never been to church. He had no knowledge of the things of God, no moral foundation in God's law.

When a couple in our church shared the good news of Jesus Christ with Shane, he responded enthusiastically and was miraculously saved. Shane's first few weeks as a Christian were marked by tremendous joy and excitement. Everything was new and wonderful! He was in love with Jesus. God had made him a new creature.

A few weeks after his salvation, Shane came to my office one day with a problem. I could tell from the look on his face that something was deeply troubling him. In all innocence he explained his concern. "Now that I am a Christian," he confided, "when I have sex with my girlfriend, I feel like the Holy Spirit is grieved!"

I quickly opened the Bible and explained to Shane how God feels about sex outside of marriage. Shane responded with sincere repentance. Shane loved the Spirit and didn't want to do anything to grieve Him.

I believe Shane's testimony is a beautiful picture of the Spirit's indwelling ministry in action. Everything in Shane's background had programmed him to accept sexual immorality as a normal part of life. No one had yet explained the Ten Commandments to Shane. He had no external moral framework by which to judge his actions; yet Shane's heart was sensitive to the indwelling Spirit, and he sensed the Spirit's displeasure with his sin. Even though he knew very little of the Word and had only been saved a few weeks, the indwelling Holy Spirit had begun the process of convicting Shane of sin and leading him on the path of righteousness.

That's the goal of the Spirit in each of our lives. As we respond to the Spirit's gentle leading, He produces in us more and more of the righteousness of Jesus. Romans 8:4 promises that the righteous requirements of the law are fully met in those who live according to the Spirit.

Since that first Easter Sunday when the glorified Christ imparted the Holy Spirit to His disciples, God's Spirit has dwelt in the heart of every believer. Romans 8:9 tells us if you don't have the Spirit indwelling you, you don't have Christ at all! *If you really know Christ, you will have His Spirit dwelling in your heart.*

When you turned to God and said, "Jesus, I need You. I place my trust in You. Forgive my sins and make me Your own," at that very moment the Spirit of God came to live in your innermost being. And He is with you always.

KEY FACTS ABOUT INDWELLING

If every Christian is indwelt by the Holy Spirit at the moment of salvation, this reveals several significant details about this work of the Spirit.

First, it tells us that the indwelling of the Spirit is *automatic.* You don't have to pray for the Spirit of God to come and live

The indwelling presence of the Holy Spirit is standard equipment for the Christian life.

within you. You don't have to *seek* His indwelling presence. You don't have to beg or plead or fast for it. It is a blessing you receive automatically as part of your salvation.

When you go to the Chevy dealer and buy a new car off the showroom floor, you don't have to ask them to install an engine. You don't have to wait for it to be installed. You don't even have to pay extra for it! The engine comes as standard equipment; it's part of the package. In the same way, the indwelling presence of the Holy Spirit is standard equipment for the Christian life.

A lot of people come to the Lord without any knowledge of the Holy Spirit. They don't know who the Spirit is. They don't ask to be indwelt. They only know they need Jesus. Yet as they respond to His invitation in repentance and faith, the Spirit of God comes to live within them. New believers frequently testify that their language has cleared up, that they don't lose their tempers the way they used to and that the Bible makes sense to them. Suddenly, they can understand the Word of God!

These men and women have never been taught about the Spirit's ministry but, like Shane, when they trusted in Jesus, something inside them changed! That's the indwelling ministry of the Spirit.

If the indwelling ministry of the Holy Spirit begins at the moment of salvation, we can also see that indwelling is *not directly experiential*. That is, when the Spirit of God comes and takes up residence within your body, there is not usually any discernible feeling or sensation associated with it.

In Cecil B. DeMille's version of *The Ten Commandments*, when Charlton Heston encountered the Spirit of God at the burning bush, he had an incredible experience. He was so immediately transformed that even his hair color changed! That is *not* usually the case with the Spirit's indwelling ministry.

When the Holy Spirit enters your innermost being you don't necessarily look different, sound different, smell different or feel different. In most cases when the Spirit initially comes, you wouldn't know anything at all had happened if you didn't read it in the Word. (As we will see, this is quite different from the empowering ministry of the Spirit.)

What we *do* experience is the fruit of the Spirit's work in our lives. As days and weeks pass, you begin to notice changes in your life as a result of the Spirit's presence. These changes generally fall into three categories: the illumination of the Word, the fruit of righteousness and the heart of Jesus increasingly expressed through your personality. Let's take a closer look at these.

ILLUMINATING THE WORD

The first thing the Holy Spirit does in the new believer's life is to bring him or her into a new relationship with the Bible. He *illumines* the Word. the word "illumine" pictures the shining of a bright light so what is present can be clearly seen. This ministry of illumination sometimes produces dramatic changes.

Sammy grew up in a Christian family and, in an effort to please his parents, tried for many years to read the Bible. Sammy was a good reader and always did well in school, but when he would try to read the Bible he found it to be a closed book. He couldn't seem to grasp what it was saying. As he tried to discipline himself to read the Word, his eyes would move from word to word, but the meaning would escape him. Time and again his attempts to read the Bible ended in frustration.

As a teenager Sammy grew more and more rebellious. He would frequently mock and ridicule his Christian parents for spending time reading the Bible. Why would *anyone* spend so much time reading such a meaningless book?

Then one summer at a Christian camp, Sammy received Jesus as Savior. The Holy Spirit came to live within his heart, and the Bible became a whole new book to him. It was as though someone had rewritten it overnight! Sammy began to spend hours every day reading this wonderful book, the verses seeming to jump off the page!

What made the difference? The Holy Spirit was supernaturally ministering the truth of the Word into his heart. What was once a dead, dry book had now become an exciting book filled with life.

Jesus described this work of the Spirit in this way:

When he, the Spirit of truth, comes, he will guide you into all truth. he will not speak on his own; he will speak only what he hears, and he will tell you what is yet to come. he will bring glory to me by taking from what is mine and making it known to you (John 16:13,14).

That was the very first result of the Spirit's indwelling ministry. Luke 24:45 tells us that when Jesus appeared to the disciples and imparted the Holy Spirit to them, He "opened their minds" to understand the Scriptures. Their minds were opened to receive and understand the things of God. The Spirit desires to do this in your life, too. He wants to open up the Bible to you so that your spirit may be fed and nourished as you grow to maturity in Christ.

THE FRUIT OF THE SPIRIT

A second work of the indwelling Holy Spirit is to implant in you the righteousness of Christ. He does this by producing *the fruit of the Spirit* in your life.

Galatians 5:22,23 shows the fruit of the Spirit to be "love, joy, peace, patience, kindness, goodness, faithfulness, gentleness and self-control." These nine qualities are very significant. Together, they describe the character of Jesus. As you read through the Gospels, you will find that His life was a perfect and balanced expression of love, joy, peace, patience, etc. Jesus is the ultimate expression of each of these spiritual traits.

These qualities also provide us a practical picture of righteousness. For a description of what it would look like to live a perfect life that never violates God's moral standard, examine these nine qualities. Remember, Jesus taught that the first of these, "love," itself fulfills all of the law and the prophets! (See Matt. 22:39.)

When the Spirit of God is allowed to produce these qualities in your daily life, you will demonstrate the righteousness of Jesus in your life. C. I. Scofield said, "Christian character is not mere moral or legal correctness, but the possession and manifestation of (these) nine graces...Taken together they present a moral portrait of Christ."[2]

I believe it's significant that Galatians 5:22 calls these nine qualities "fruit." Fruit is not something you have to force or strain to produce. A fruit tree doesn't have to struggle and strive to bear fruit; it just grows.

That's how it is with the fruit of the Spirit.

You don't have to struggle or exercise great amounts of self-discipline to produce them. If you yield to the Spirit and are growing in Him, this fruit will be naturally produced in your life. As you grow in the Spirit, you will find that it is easier to love than it used to be. You will tend to be more joyful. You will discover greater peace in your heart and mind. You won't lose your temper like you used to. That's the fruit of the Spirit growing in your life.

MOTIVATIONAL GIFTS OF THE SPIRIT

Another way the indwelling Spirit changes you is by expressing the *heart* of Jesus through your personality.

When Jesus walked through this earth, His heart was deeply troubled by sin and its effects. When He saw sin, He was moved with the zeal of God to correct it (see John 2:14-17). When He saw physical hunger, He was moved to compassion and fed the multitudes (see Matt. 15:32). When He saw pain, His heart was stirred to minister comfort and healing (see Matt. 14:14). When He saw the multitudes in confusion, "like sheep without a shepherd," He had compassion on them and taught them many things (see Mark 6:34).

One of the ways the Holy Spirit wants to make you like Jesus is to place the desires of Jesus' heart into *your* heart, so that, in a measure, you are motivated by the things that motivated Him.

These expressions of the heart of Jesus are often called *motivational gifts*. They are God-given desires to respond to needs in specific ways. These motivational gifts are listed in Romans 12:3-8.

Prophecy. In this context, prophecy is not the ability to receive messages from God. It's a prophetic *motivation* to correct error by revealing the will of God in a given situation. A person with a prophetic motivational gift quickly discerns when something is wrong and has a deep desire to correct it.

Serving. The gift of serving is an expression of Jesus' desire to minister to the practical needs of others.

Teaching. The gift of teaching is a God-given desire to communicate the truth of God in order to give enablement and direction.

Encouraging. This is a God-given motivation to motivate and encourage others in the Lord.

Giving. Giving is a deeply implanted desire to sacrificially give in tangible ways to meet the needs of others.

Leading. Leading is the ability and desire to give people a vision of what God wants done and effectively coordinate their efforts to accomplish it.

Mercy. This is an expression of the compassion of Jesus toward the grieving and wounded, a desire to strengthen and heal those in need.

As a Christian, you are called to minister in all these ways, but the Spirit of God has given you *one* of these gifts as the basic motivation of your life.

As you grow in the Lord and seek to serve Him, you will discover that you tend to be a giver, a server, a leader, a teacher, etc. All that you do for the Lord will be shaped and colored by the motivational gift placed within you by the indwelling Spirit. The end result of this gifting is that Jesus is able to express His heart—and reveal Himself—through you.

A KEY QUESTION

If the Spirit of God is placed within every Christian to produce godly character, why is it that so many Christians don't exhibit godly character?

We all know Christians who don't act much different from unbelievers. Why is it that the lives of some people have been totally transformed by the Spirit, while others don't seem to change at all? When we examine our own lives, we discover that we are often guilty of actions that are not pleasing to a holy God! Why doesn't the indwelling Spirit change us in those areas?

To understand why a person who is a "temple of the Holy Spirit" (1 Cor. 6:19) can still live in sin, we need to see how the indwelling ministry of the Spirit operates. We will look at this process in the next chapter.

3

TRANSFORMED BY THE SPIRIT

Paul looked down at the letter in his hand and again shook his head. It had been three weeks since the courier had brought the letter from Corinth and it still weighed heavily on him.

He kept asking himself, How could the things reported in this letter be true? Could the Christians of Corinth really be doing the kinds of things this letter describes? *Yet the still, small voice of the Spirit of God within him bore witness to what the letter said.*

Here was a whole church, several hundred people, who claimed to love Jesus. Yet, their lifestyles bespoke a people little different from the pagans that surrounded them in the wicked city of Corinth.

The letter described a church full of strife and factions: Christians full of hatred and anger toward each other; Christians taking other Christians to court and suing them before unbelieving judges; Christians engaged in sexual immorality; Christians misusing the gifts of the Holy Spirit; Christians actually getting drunk at the Lord's Table!

Paul didn't have any doubt these people were saved. He had personally led many of them to Christ. He had spent time with them, praying for them and nurturing them through the first few months of their life with Jesus.

When he left Corinth to continue his missionary journey, Paul had given them specific instructions on how to grow in the Lord. But somehow they had missed it. Instead of growing to maturity as men and women of God, these Christians were still acting like unbelievers!

The apostle John would write that he had no greater joy than seeing his children walking in the truth. Paul discovered the opposite is also true. There was very little that distressed him more than seeing his spiritual children walking in sin.

For three weeks his heart had been burdened for the Corinthians. He recognized well the weight in his spirit that indicated a call to intercession. All through the day he would pray and fast for them. In the middle of the night he would wake to find these wayward brothers and sisters on his mind. If there had been any way possible, he would have left the work in Ephesus and rushed to Corinth to deal with the problem himself, but he knew he could not.

As he reread the letter one more time, he sensed the Spirit of God speaking to him. Taking a parchment and quill, he quickly began to write down what the Spirit was saying. It was a letter to the Corinthians. He wrote, "Paul...to the church of God in Corinth..."

As the Spirit directed, Paul began to address some of the problems in the Corinthian church. Then, in a moment of revelation, the Spirit showed him their root problem....

When Paul wrote his first letter to the Corinthians, he not only dealt with the pressing problems of a carnal church, but he also gave us a clear explanation of how the indwelling Spirit desires to operate in our lives.

The root problem in Corinth was that the Holy Spirit had not been given the freedom to accomplish His work in these Christians. They were indwelt by the Spirit, but the Spirit had been unable to produce the character of Jesus in them.

FOUR KINDS OF PEOPLE

In his letter to the Corinthians, Paul diagnosed the problem. In chapters 2 and 3 he deals with four different kinds of people: the natural man, the spiritual man, infants in Christ and worldly Christians.

NATURAL PEOPLE

> The man without the Spirit does not accept the things that come from the Spirit of God, for they are foolishness to him, and he cannot understand them, because they are spiritually discerned (1 Cor. 2:14).

The *natural person* is an unbeliever. He does not have the Holy Spirit dwelling within him. When he reads the Bible there is no one to illumine it. It's just "words on a page." He does not understand spiritual truth. His life is in darkness; his flesh is in control. The works of the flesh are evident in his life (see Gal. 5:19-21).

That's what the Corinthians had been like before they were saved, and that is also what you and I were like without Jesus!

Sometimes I hear Christians criticizing or condemning unbelievers for their sin. That's like criticizing a zebra for having stripes! An unbeliever sins because he is a sinner. His spirit is cut off from God and his soul is in darkness. He has no option but to sin. He doesn't need us to criticize and condemn him. What he needs is the impartation of the life of God that only comes through God's free gift of salvation.

SPIRITUAL CHRISTIANS

> The spiritual man makes judgments about all things, but he himself is not subject to any man's judgment: "for who

65

has known the mind of the Lord that he may instruct him?" But we have the mind of Christ (1 Cor. 2:15,16).

Paul calls this person the *spiritual person*. The spiritual person is a mature Christian who has so yielded her life to the Spirit's working that the Holy Spirit reigns over every part of her life. She is able to receive and appropriate spiritual truth. The fruit of the Spirit is evident in her life. If we look closely at this person, we get a good picture of what Jesus was like.

This should be the goal of every Christian. The spiritual Christian is not sinless, but sin no longer dominates his life. He has become so sensitive to the Spirit and so responsive to His gentle leading that the righteousness of Christ can flow freely through his life.

"BABY" CHRISTIANS

Brothers, I could not address you as spiritual [persons] but as worldly—mere infants in Christ. I gave you milk, not solid food, for you were not yet ready for it (1 Cor. 3:1,2).

In this verse, Paul looks back to the time he lived and ministered among the Corinthians. Then, they had been Christians only a short time. Though they were no longer natural people, or unbelievers, they were not yet spiritual people either. They were still very young in the Lord, "infants in Christ."

The Spirit of God was indwelling them, and they were able to receive *some* truth. But they still lived their lives like natural men in many respects.

Paul fed these new Christians "spiritual milk," a few foundational teachings about the Christian life, because they were not yet ready for anything more advanced. The key to what

Paul says here is that this was a *normal* situation for a new convert. You don't expect a lot from a baby.

When my children were babies, they were not very neat eaters. It was sometimes embarrassing to take them to a restaurant. By the time they finished eating, the floor around the high chair would be covered with food. While we didn't enjoy the dirty looks we sometimes got from waiters, we couldn't be overly upset with our kids. It's *natural* for a baby to make a mess! We knew that as we trained and nurtured them, they would grow in maturity and, hopefully, become neater eaters. (Sure enough, now that twenty years have passed and they are all fine young adults, they hardly ever make a mess in the restaurant!)

A baby cannot act like an adult, nor can an infant understand what an adult can understand. God doesn't expect a brand-new Christian to act like a mature believer, either. God is not upset with a baby for being a baby, because He knows that as a baby feeds on good food, he will grow and mature.

WORLDLY, WILLFUL CHRISTIANS

Indeed, you are still not ready [for solid food]. You are still worldly. For since there is jealousy and quarreling among you, are you not worldly? Are you not acting like mere men? (1 Cor. 3:2,3).

At the time Paul is writing this letter, two years have passed since he left the city of Corinth. The Corinthians have had time to grow. By this time they should be maturing, taking on more and more of the character of Christ. They should be ready to understand some of the deeper truths of God's Word.

But they have failed to grow. They *still* are not able to receive solid food, and they are still making messes!

Paul says they are still worldly, or fleshly. Even though they have the Spirit of God within them, they are still acting like mere men. Something is wrong. The Corinthians have willfully refused to submit to the Spirit and allow Him to produce His changes in their lives.

This fourth kind of Christian is a *willful Christian*. The willful Christian still has the Holy Spirit in his life. He has been a Christian long enough to grow, but has resisted the Spirit. He lives much like a natural person, his life characterized by sin and defeat. He is one of the most miserable creatures on the face of the earth.

If he is ever to be released from his misery and become useful in God's kingdom, either he must choose to repent or God will bring tribulation into his life to break him of his willfulness.

I believe every individual falls into one of these four categories. You are either

FOUR KINDS OF PEOPLE

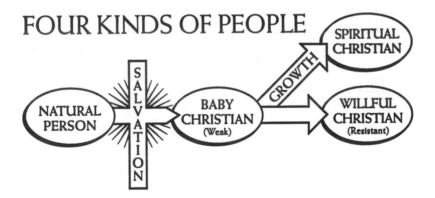

a *natural person*, who has never trusted in Jesus;

a *weak "baby" Christian*, who has trusted Jesus but has either lacked the time or teaching necessary to grow in the Lord;

a *willful, carnal Christian*, who has resisted the Spirit's attempts to change you; or

a *spiritual Christian*, who continues to grow and become more and more like Jesus.

WHAT MAKES THE DIFFERENCE?

That's the question. How do we start as weak Christians and grow to spiritual maturity? What is necessary for the indwelling Spirit to accomplish His work?

If the indwelling Spirit is to accomplish His work in you, two things are required from you: (1) You must have a *repentant heart* and (2) you must *feed on the Word.* If you do this, the Spirit of God will have the freedom to build you to maturity and produce in you the godly character of Jesus.

REPENTANCE

The first action required for spiritual growth is *repentance*, something most Christians don't talk much about anymore. Bob Mumford describes the kind of "gospel message" many people today preach as "God is a good God. The Devil is a bad devil. Come to Jesus and He'll be your head butler!"

Irreverent? Perhaps. But it's all too descriptive of the "good news" many evangelists proclaim. "Ask Jesus into your life and He'll fix all your problems. You don't have to change. You don't have' to give up anything! He loves you so much, He'll make you healthy, wealthy and happy if you'll just say this little prayer right now." That's the message far too many sinners are hearing.

What happened to turning away from sin? Where's the teaching on dying to your old life? Without repentance, people try to turn *to* Jesus without turning *from* the world. They try to fashion a Christian life without one of the most important ingredients: a repentant heart.

Because of this, Christians are cheated out of the opportunity to experience what God wants them to enjoy. They never experience the love and joy and fulfillment Jesus offers. They can't experience many of the resources of the Holy Spirit because they've neglected the very first requirement.

The starting point of a walk with God is *always* repentance.

John the Baptist said, "*Repent*, for the kingdom of heaven is near" (Matt. 3:2).

Jesus said, "*Repent*, for the kingdom of heaven is near" (Matt. 4:17).

Peter said, "*Repent* and be baptized, every one of you" (Acts 2:38).

Paul echoed their sentiments: "God...commands all people everywhere to *repent*" (Acts 17:30).

The Bible consistently teaches that the first requirement for knowing God is repentance, but what does it mean to repent? Many think of repentance only as "turning from sin." That is a *part* of repentance, but there is more to it than that. Here's a more complete definition:

Repentance is turning *from* everything you used to seek life from, and turning *to* Jesus as the source of your life.

The Bible teaches that we need to repent of *anything* we cling to as a source of life outside of Jesus.

For "sinners," repentance means turning from sin (see Matt. 4:17).

For idolaters, it means turning from idols (see 1 Cor. 5:10).

For the Pharisees, it meant turning from their law and tradition (see Matt. 19:3-6).

For the rich young ruler, it meant turning from material possessions (see Matt. 19:21).

For the religious person who thinks his good deeds will get him to heaven, repentance means turning from the "dead works" of human righteousness (see Heb. 6:1).

Most people come to God loaded down with all the things in which they've tried to find life. I like to picture these things as a huge pile of trash we carry around on our backs. For some, this pile consists of wealth and possessions. For some it may be various kinds of sin and perversion. For some the pile is made up of religious activities and church involvement. For others it's a sport or a hobby, or even some intangible thing like success or popularity. It's all of the things we have trusted in to impart life to us.

Then we encounter Jesus and His offer of LIFE. We recognize that we have not found life in the things of this world, so we try to reach out with one hand, grab hold of Jesus, and add Him to our pile!

HOW WE TRY TO COME TO JESUS

We try to make Jesus one more interest, one more activity, one more category in life. We get out our schedules and find a convenient time slot for Jesus to occupy. We "fit Him in," just as we would a baseball game or a tennis match. And then we wonder why the Christian life doesn't "work."

But Jesus never agreed to walk with us on those terms. He refuses to be just one interest among many. He is not satisfied to be just "one more god" in the pantheon of my interests. He wants it ALL. Jesus wants me to deal with the fact that I *belong to Him.* He bought me with His blood. "You are not your own; you were bought at a price" (1 Cor. 6:19,20). He wants me to lay down my life, to offer my body as a living sacrifice to Him (see Rom. 12:1,2). He asks me to drop my huge pile of trash at the foot of the Cross and cling to Him alone.

That's repentance!

Once I've repented, I may still have my friends and hobbies and possessions. But my life doesn't depend on those things anymore. I can turn from them in a moment if He asks me to.

That isn't just nice religious talk. It isn't just theoretical. There *are* times when God *will* ask you to turn away from things that have been very special to you.

When I was growing up, I wanted to be a doctor. I never wanted to be a policeman or a fireman or an astronaut. Whenever anyone asked me what I wanted to be, I told them without hesitation, "I'm going to be a doctor." I planned my life around it. I loved to study chemistry and biology. I would watch TV documentaries and read books about medicine.

I was in my second year in premed at the University of South Florida when I felt God say, "I have something different for you. I want you to minister for Me." At first I was crushed. How could God ask that? I loved God, but I didn't want to be a pastor. I wanted to be a doctor. I struggled with it for several weeks, but within a month, my major was changed and my whole life turned in a different direction.

God has the right to do that! And if you really love Him, you won't regret it.

Paul's testimony was that he lost *everything* to gain Christ. Paul had been the rising star in Judaism. He was a Pharisee of the Pharisees with a respected genealogy. He had studied under

REPENTANCE

the great rabbi Gamaliel and knew the Old Testament Scriptures as well as anyone in his day. He had a secure future before him as a religious leader with recognition and respect.

Then Jesus appeared to him, and he threw it all away. He took all of the things he had counted as gain, and chose to count them as rubbish. He "suffered the loss of all things" to gain Jesus (Phil. 3:8, *NASB*). And he found that Jesus was worth it!

Paul discovered what millions of others have found down through history: When we turn from everything else and cling to Jesus, we find that Jesus satisfies as nothing else can! That's the attitude we need to have to walk with God. Repentance means we give ourselves so *totally* to Jesus that anything that interferes with our fellowship with Him is laid at the foot of the Cross without hesitation.

I'd like to suggest that you stop right now and make sure you have taken this crucial step. Make a list of the things you have turned to in your attempts to find life. Be sure to include things like hobbies, interests, people, recreational activities, work and talents. Ask yourself, *Have I laid these things at the foot of the Cross and left them there? Am I relying totally on Jesus for my life, or am I trying to add Jesus as just one more item in the pile?*

If you are not sure you have repented of these things, I urge you to do it right now. Here's a sample prayer of repentance:

Dear Lord, right now I choose to lay these things down at Your feet. (Read the things you have listed.) I choose to give these things to You. I want to cling to You and draw my life and my satisfaction from You!

I consciously, as an act of my will, choose to present my body to You as a living sacrifice. I give You the right to direct my life into Your good and perfect plan. Take me. Guide me. Direct me, and use me for Your purposes in this world. I pray this in Jesus' name. Amen.

Now you have taken the first step in walking with God. If you maintain that heart attitude of repentance, being always willing to change in response to the Holy Spirit's prompting, the indwelling Holy Spirit will have freedom to accomplish His work in you.

FEEDING ON THE WORD

If you want the indwelling Spirit of God to continue producing His work in your life, you must also feed on the Word.

Paul reminded the Corinthians that while he was with them he gave them the nourishment they needed to grow. "I gave you milk, not solid food, for you were not yet ready for it" (1 Cor. 3:2). When the Corinthians were infants in Christ, Paul ministered to them by feeding them spiritual food they were able to receive, chew and digest.

Babies mature into adults, both in the natural realm and the spiritual realm, by taking in good, nourishing food and growing. The food we need for spiritual growth is the Word of God.

The Bible is not an ordinary book. It is a spiritual book. Its very words are supernaturally inspired by the Holy Spirit. As we read, study and meditate on the Word, the indwelling Spirit of

---

As you obey the leadings of the Holy Spirit, His power is released in your life and sin's dominion is broken.

God energizes the words of this Book to release life into our innermost being. That is how we receive spiritual nourishment. We are instructed in 1 Peter 2:2 that, like newborn babes, we should long for the pure milk of the Word, so that by it we can "grow up" in our salvation.

Of course, it's not enough just to read the Bible. We need to study and meditate on the Bible, saturating our minds with it. We should long for it and hunger for it, but most of all, we need to submit our lives to it. We must come to the Word with a repentant heart.

As the Spirit of God illumines the Word to you, He will show you the areas in your life He wants to deal with. He reveals sins you need to repent of. As you obey His leadings, His power is released and sin's dominion is broken. You begin to grow to maturity, and the character of Jesus is manifested in your life.

If you want a formula for spiritual growth, I believe this is it:

FEEDING ON GOD'S WORD + REPENTANCE = GROWTH

As we hunger after the Bible and yield to the Spirit, we will grow to spiritual maturity. The Spirit of God takes the seed of the Word, plants it in the soil of a repentant heart, and from it springs the fruit of the Spirit. That's the indwelling ministry of the Spirit!

Can the Holy Spirit really change a life from the inside and break the power and defilement of sin? Allow me to share a true-life testimony of the ministry of the indwelling Spirit.

One of the most respected leaders in the Church today is Chuck D. Pierce, vice president of Global Harvest Ministries and executive director of the World Prayer Center. I have had the privilege of knowing Chuck as a close friend and coworker for more than ten years. He is a loving and godly father to his family and one of the most powerfully gifted ministers I have ever encountered.

While Chuck is known internationally as a conference speaker, author and prayer leader, many don't know his background. Chuck grew up in a highly dysfunctional family. His father was an alcoholic and gambler who gambled away the family's sizable inheritance. While his mother struggled to hold the family together, his dad drifted from one adulterous relationship to another. As Chuck moved into his teenage years, his father subjected him to increasingly severe levels of emotional and physical abuse.

As a pastor, I've found that people who have endured heavy abuse are often scarred for life. Abused children become angry adults filled with bitterness and resentment, and they often become trapped in the same lifestyle practiced by the parent that abused them. Chuck's background was as bad as that of anyone I've known, yet somehow Chuck escaped this destructive cycle. How did Chuck escape the defilement of his background and go on to become a godly Christian leader?

Although Chuck came to know Jesus as a child, by the time he graduated from high school he had already begun to follow the destructive example of his father. Even though he hated the things his father had done, Chuck found himself doing much of the same. He pursued a path of destruction for eighteen months until he finally suffered a physical collapse and ended up in the hospital with double pneumonia. By the grace of God, Chuck was put in a room with a Pentecostal preacher for two weeks. As that preacher shared the Lord with him, Chuck began to repent. In that hospital room, Chuck read *The Cross and the Switchblade* and then began to read the Bible.

As he read the Bible, God began to speak to him. There came a point when God came down into that hospital room and gave Chuck this promise: "I will restore to you that which you have lost."

As Chuck continued to read the Word, God began to turn his life around. When Chuck was 24 years old, God took him to Romans 6:14 where he read, "Sin shall not have dominion over you" (KJV).

Chuck asked the Lord, "Is this true?"

God answered in an *audible* voice, "Yes!"

Chuck asked, "Is the rest of this Book true?"

Again God answered, "Yes!"

Chuck determined from that point not to rationalize his sin or excuse it any longer. He would submit to the Lord and allow God to bring his life into obedience to the Word.

Since that day, for the last 25 years, Chuck has read through the entire Bible at least once, sometimes twice each year. He rises early in the morning and daily saturates his mind with God's Word. As Chuck reads the Word, he is committed to obeying what God tells him.

God has told Chuck to do some difficult things, to give up things that were very precious to him. But the result has been that the indwelling Holy Spirit has had great freedom to produce the character of Christ within his heart. The vicious cycle of sin and destruction was broken from Chuck Pierce's life.

People who hear Chuck minister frequently ask how the power and revelation of God flows so freely through him. The answer is that Chuck has allowed the indwelling Spirit to transform his life and produce in him a purified vessel. That's what the Spirit desires to accomplish in *every* believer.

The indwelling Spirit is *always* ready to do His work in our lives. He is looking for men and women who will yield their lives to Him with repentant hearts and feed their spirits the food of His Word so that the transforming work of the Spirit can be accomplished.

If you are spending time in the Word of God, searching it with a humble heart and allowing the Spirit to apply it to your life, you *will* grow from being a weak Christian to become a spiritual Christian.

INDWELLING VS. EMPOWERING

It's important to note that the Spirit's *indwelling* work takes place totally apart from the *empowering* work of the Spirit. It is possible to have great empowering and to function in all the supernatural ministry gifts, while at the same time resisting the work of the Spirit to mature you.

The Christians at Corinth are a good example of this. The Corinthian Christians had received the empowering of the Spirit and were functioning in the Spirit's supernatural gifts. They demonstrated great power! They regularly spoke in tongues. Miracles and healings were a common occurrence among them. Yet they were not mature. God said that in their character, despite all the supernatural manifestations, they were not spiritual, but still fleshly or carnal.

There are some Christians like that today. They have been equipped by God to operate in great power, but they are not mature. They place very little emphasis on learning God's Word. The result is they accomplish very little for Jesus. They wield a lot of power, but they lack the maturity to use it effectively.

We must emphasize the teaching of the Bible and the necessity of growing to maturity. I urge you to commit yourself to study God's Word, submit to it, and allow God's indwelling Spirit to grow you to maturity and give you the character of Christ.

EMPOWERED BY THE SPIRIT, EQUIPPED TO SERVE

Richard and Greg sat cross-legged on the packed mud-and-dung floor of the dingy hut. The air reeked of decay, sweat and urine, but they had long since ceased to notice the pungent aromas of the native village. Their attention was fixed on the shriveled old man who sat facing them across the ashes of the fire pit. As village chief, the old man usually spoke with a confident authority, knowing his words were respected by everyone in the village. Yet as he spoke with them now, his words seemed frail and halting, almost pathetic. As Richard and Greg heard his explanation and sensed the fear in the old chief's tired eyes, they were honestly perplexed.

Both Richard and Greg were godly young missionaries with a sincere desire to serve Jesus. They had graduated from a major evangelical seminary where they learned to teach the Bible and apply it to the practical needs of people. Both had sensed a clear call to missions and had felt the Lord direct them to bring the gospel to a particularly dark area of Africa.

They had raised their support, gone through language school and pioneered a new work "where no missionary had gone before."

At first their ministry efforts looked promising. When they established their first Bible study, the natives seemed genuinely enthusiastic. A large percentage of the village attended, including the chief and many of the tribal elders. Yet now, as they drew near the end of their first term in the field, their entire ministry was falling apart. Attendance had dwindled, and many of the natives would no longer speak with them. Had they somehow offended them? Had they broken some cultural taboo?

They finally persuaded the chief to meet with them to discuss the problem, but they were in no way prepared for the explanation the old man gave.

"No, you did not offend us," the chief assured them. "We all greatly enjoyed your Bible studies."

"But what is the problem then? Do you not believe the things we teach you?" Richard pressed.

"We believe the things you teach are true," the chief responded, almost in tears, "but you have given us no way to deal with the demons that torture and torment us all night long whenever we attend your meetings!"

Soon after their meeting with the chief, the young men returned home from the mission field in defeat and never returned. These godly young men were well trained to teach the Bible, but they were not equipped to successfully combat the powers of darkness they encountered in that village.

These two missionaries encountered a frustration that many ministers in the United States also experience. There are times when ministry training, education and hard work are not enough. These are times when only the *supernatural power of God* will get results.

Whether the problem is a man so tormented by demons that he wants to take his own life, a young mother who has just been diagnosed with cancer, or a person so emotionally crippled he cannot function in a normal relationship, there are problems against which our best human efforts prove totally ineffective.

POWER FOR MINISTRY

In the New Testament, the solution to problems like these is found in the *anointing* of God. The apostles could not be deterred from their ministry by the powers of darkness. When diabolical forces or difficult circumstances came against them, the apostles responded with a demonstration of God's power to heal the sick, cast out demons and set the captives free (see Acts 3:2-10; 16:16-18, 23-28). As a result, the Church grew and prospered.

In the book of Acts, the apostles repeatedly met with strong opposition. In one instance, Peter and John were arrested, jailed, threatened and ordered to cease their preaching. How did they respond? They joined together in earnest prayer for the *power* of the Spirit to be released in healings and miracles (see Acts 4:30). The miracles that followed brought such opportunity for witness that they quickly filled Jerusalem with their teaching (see Acts 5:15,16,28).

In the same way, the power of the Spirit opens doors for ministry today. It does this, first, by *removing obstacles* that would hinder God's people in their service. My good friend Marty Waldman is a Messianic Jew who came to know *Yeshua* (Jesus) in the midst of the Jesus Movement. As the call of God on his life became evident, Satan moved to frustrate that call; Marty developed a medical condition that left him totally blind.

Fortunately, Marty was part of a fellowship that was willing to pray for his healing. The elders of the congregation came together and prayed for him, anointing him with oil in obedience to James 5:14,15. He was *instantly* healed and his sight restored. What could have been a major impediment to God's call was removed, and Marty has gone on to head one of the largest Messianic Jewish congregations in the nation.

The demonstrated power of the Spirit not only removes hindrances to ministry, it also convinces the lost of the truth of our message. In his book *Praying with Power*, Dr. C. Peter Wagner gives an example of how God's power is bringing whole villages to the Lord in China. An evangelist named Brother Yeng was holding an evangelistic meeting in a village where the gospel had never been preached, when some local gangsters arrived to disrupt the meeting. As Brother Yeng saw the situation developing, he quietly prayed for God to demonstrate His power in a miraculous way. Dr. Wagner describes God's response:

> Sensing the flow of the Holy Spirit's power in answer to his prayer, Brother Yeng boldly said, "Is anyone here deaf?" A woman came forward bringing a deaf woman, who obviously had not heard the question. Brother Yeng prayed that God would heal the deaf woman, and she was immediately healed! He then invited all others who were deaf to come forward, and, by God's grace, every one of them was healed right before the eyes of the audience.[1]

People began to go out and get their sick family members and bring them to the meeting. Before the end of the night, six paralyzed people also were healed. The gangsters were so amazed by what was happening, they went home and brought back their sick family members, too! That night, because of the miracles, the whole village—including the gangsters—came to Christ.

This account is typical of what God is doing in mission fields all over the world. The majority of China's 50 to 75 million believers have come to faith in Jesus as a result of witnessing the miraculous power of God. Deng Zhaoming, editor of the ecumenical Chinese magazine *Bridge* and a distinguished China watcher comments, "In the church of China, at least 50 percent of believers became Christians through a remarkable healing taking place in their family."[2]

That's the New Testament pattern of ministry! In Romans 15:19, Paul states that he led men and women to the Lord "by the power of signs and miracles, through the power of the

Spirit." Paul did not rely on his human intellect to convince men of the gospel. His apologetic was the demonstration of the Holy Spirit's *power*, so that his listeners' faith "might not rest on men's wisdom, but on God's power" (1 Cor. 2:5).

The same Holy Spirit who empowered Paul's ministry is

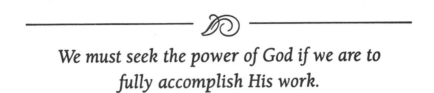

We must seek the power of God if we are to fully accomplish His work.

available and ready to aid God's people today. Wherever Christians are willing to embrace His empowering ministry, there is always a dramatic increase in effectiveness.

Jesus went so far as to warn His disciples not to begin their ministry until they had been *clothed with power* from on high (see Luke 24:49). Even though the indwelling Spirit is present within us, we must also seek the power of God if we are to fully accomplish His work.

WHAT IS EMPOWERING?

The empowering of the Holy Spirit is the ministry by which the Spirit of God "comes upon" you with power to equip you for supernatural ministry.

Simply put, the empowering of the Spirit is an experience that *equips* you with supernatural resources to accomplish the work of God. His power enables you to do the very works of Christ, as He promised in John 14:12: "He that believeth on me, the works that I do shall he do also; and greater works than these shall he do; because I go unto my Father" (*KJV*).

The empowering of the Spirit is called by many different names. Many call it the "baptism of the Holy Spirit" (see Matt. 3:11). Others call it being "filled by the Spirit" (see Acts 2:4). Still others speak in terms of receiving "divine unction" or "the anointing." The Bible frequently refers to the Spirit "coming upon" a person, being "poured out" on a person (Acts 2:33) or simply being "on" a person (Acts 1:8).

We must be careful not to get bogged down in terminology. If you don't like one name, use a different one. *The important thing is not the name; it's the power.* We need the power of God if we are to be effective in doing the work of God.

THE AVAILABILITY OF GOD'S POWER

Unlike the indwelling ministry of the Holy Spirit, His empowering ministry is not limited to the New Testament age. Many examples are found in the Old Testament of the Spirit *coming upon* people in the same way He does today (see Judg. 3:9-11; 1 Sam. 10:1-11 and others).

Consider the following example from the book of Numbers:

> The Lord said to Moses: "Bring me seventy of Israel's elders.... Have them come to the Tent of Meeting, that they may stand there with you. I will come down and speak with you there, and I will take of the Spirit that is on you and put the Spirit on them. They will help you carry the burden of the people so that you will not have to carry it alone.
>
> So Moses went out and...brought together seventy of their elders and had them stand around the Tent. Then the Lord came down in the cloud and spoke with him, and he took of the Spirit that was on him and put the Spirit on the seventy elders. When the Spirit rested on them, they prophesied and continued to do so. [See *NIV* text note.]

However, two men, whose names were Eldad and Medad, had remained in the camp. They were listed among the elders, but did not go out to the Tent. Yet the Spirit also rested on them, and they prophesied in the camp. A young man ran and told Moses, "Eldad and Medad are prophesying in the camp."

Joshua son of Nun, who had been Moses' aide since youth, spoke up and said, "Moses, my lord, stop them!"

But Moses replied, "Are you jealous for my sake? I wish that all the Lord's people were prophets and that the Lord would put his Spirit on them!" (Num. 11:16,17,24-29).

This account relates an encounter with the Holy Spirit very similar to that described in the book of Acts. The Spirit of God came upon individuals to equip and empower them, and the evidence was a supernatural manifestation of prophesying. This kind of ministry of the Spirit is very different from His indwelling ministry, but it is well documented in both the Old and New Testaments.

Moses expressed his desire that this ministry could be available to all of God's people, but in Old Testament times this ministry was limited. Only a "chosen few" were given the privilege of receiving the Spirit's empowering.

Yet God promised the time would come when the empowering work of the Holy Spirit *would be* available to all. In the book of Joel, God assures us, "Afterward, I will pour out my Spirit on all people. Your sons and daughters will prophesy, your old men will dream dreams, your young men will see visions. Even on my servants, both men and women, I will pour out my Spirit in those days" (Joel 2:28,29).

In Peter's sermon on the day of Pentecost, he declared the time spoken of by Joel had arrived (see Acts 2:16-18). The empowering of the Holy Spirit is now available to *all* of God's people.

We are living in a day when every Christian, old and young, man or woman, can experience the supernatural empowering of the Holy Spirit. Unfortunately, while the power of the Spirit is available to all Christians, not all Christians experience this power.

RECEIVING HIS POWER

The *indwelling* ministry of the Spirit is automatic. You don't have to ask the Spirit to live inside you. You don't have to seek His indwelling presence. He came and took up residence within your heart at the moment of your salvation.

In contrast, the *empowering* of the Spirit is seldom automatic, usually coming instead in response to prayer. Let's look at a few New Testament examples of individuals receiving the Spirit's empowering.

THE DISCIPLES

The disciples were indwelt by the Spirit on the day Jesus rose from the grave (see John 20:22). More than a month and a half later, on the day of Pentecost, the disciples were empowered by the Spirit. On that day, the Holy Spirit responded to weeks of prayer and intercession by coming upon them in power (see Acts 2).

THE SAMARITANS

In Acts 8, many Samaritans were saved when Philip preached in Samaria. (We know from Romans 8 that when they received Christ, they were indwelt by the Holy Spirit.) It was not until several days later when Peter and John came and laid hands on the Samaritans that they were filled, or empowered, with the Spirit.

PAUL

Paul was converted on the road to Damascus (see Acts 9:5). When he trusted in Jesus he was indwelt by the Holy Spirit. Three days later a disciple named Ananias came, laid hands on him and prayed for him to be empowered by the Spirit (see Acts 9:17).

Each of these examples reflects the normal experience of the early Christians. In most biblical accounts, the empowering of the Spirit takes place not at the time of salvation, but shortly after salvation. And it comes in response to specific prayer.

Augustine tells us that in his day (the fourth century) it was the practice for new converts to be brought before the church. The elders of the church would then lay hands on the new believers and pray for them to be filled with the Holy Spirit.

Because the empowering of the Spirit does not usually take place automatically, we must learn how to receive it and how to walk in it. In the next chapter we will look at the basic principles for receiving the power of the Holy Spirit.

RECEIVING HIS POWER...
AND PASSING IT ON

*"You've got to help me!" the voice on the phone pleaded, "There's got to
be more to the Christian life than what I'm experiencing! If this is all
there is, I don't want it anymore!" He paused a moment, then continued
almost apologetically. "I don't even know why I'm calling you, but as
I've prayed I just had a feeling that you would have an answer for me."*

*The speaker on the phone had been one of my best friends during
my days at seminary. Although not a seminary student himself, Ben
was one of the most knowledgeable Christians I knew. A highly
intelligent man, the shelves in his living room were lined with the
works of the great Protestant theologians.*

*Ben liked nothing better than to argue some obscure theological
point, and he had the knowledge to do it well. But he was not calling
me to argue theology this time. He had reached a point in his life
where an "intellectual" faith no longer satisfied. He sensed there
was a reality to the Christian life that went beyond knowing the
right doctrines, and he was desperate to find it.*

*Although he lived in a city less than an hour's drive from mine,
I had not seen Ben for several years, so I was surprised when he
chose to call me for help in this time of desperation. What Ben had
no way of knowing was that the Holy Spirit had done His work of
renewal in my life less than a year earlier.*

Ben and I set up a time to meet, and I shared with him my testimony of how the Spirit of God had recently worked in my life. He responded like a kid in a candy store. He wanted to experience the empowering of the Spirit himself! I shared with Ben what little I knew about the work of the Spirit, and he was ready for me to pray for him to be filled.

I suggested that he confess any known sins, we sang a few praise songs, and as he sat on the couch in his living room, I laid my hand on his head and prayed for him to be filled with the Spirit. We sat there in silence for a few moments…and absolutely nothing happened.

I could tell Ben was very disappointed and, frankly, so was I. I had seen the Spirit of God do a great work in my life, and I had hoped God would do something similar for Ben.

We talked for a while longer and I got up to leave. As we stood at the door, I experienced a strange sensation. I sensed in my spirit that the Holy Spirit of God had come and was "resting" on Ben, ready to do something.

Awkwardly, I said, "Ben, I sense the Holy Spirit on you right now. I think we need to go back and pray one more time."

We went back into his living room, and he again sat down on his couch. Once again, I laid my hand on his head and asked the Holy Spirit to come and fill Ben.

This time something began to happen. Ben suddenly began to breathe very deeply and tremble all over. He leaned back on the couch and seemed to go into a kind of trance. From time to time he would groan or mumble a prayer like, "Oh, dear Jesus!"

This went on for twenty minutes and, to be honest, I was a little frightened. First of all, this was totally out of character for Ben. He was an intellectual. I had never known him to be an emotionally demonstrative person.

Also, I had never personally experienced or even seen anything like this before…ever! Nothing like this had happened when the Spirit of God touched me. I honestly worried that Ben was having *some kind of breakdown. My one consolation was that I heard the Spirit of God telling me, "It's all right. This is Me."*

When Ben finally came out of it, he was so excited! He said that it had felt like the Spirit of God was peeling away layer after layer, penetrating down into his innermost being and changing him. It was the most wonderful thing he had ever experienced!

Then Ben began to prophesy. As we sat there together, the Holy Spirit began to tell him things he had no way of knowing. Ben prophesied things about me and about my ministry that were 100 percent accurate! I had never witnessed anything like it before.

Ben's experience with the Holy Spirit was not a cure-all. Ben has gone through some difficult times since this experience. But anyone who knew Ben before will testify that in many ways he is now a different person. He has had an experiential encounter with the Spirit of the living God. The power of God has been poured out upon him, and the supernatural gifts of the Spirit have begun to operate in his life. He will never be the same.

KEY FACTS ABOUT EMPOWERING

Since that evening in Ben's living room, I have prayed for a great many people to receive the empowering of the Holy Spirit. Many have had dramatic experiences. Others have just felt a sense of peace and the presence of the Spirit. Some have spoken in tongues. A few have prophesied. But for almost all, there was a major transformation of life brought about by the empowering Spirit of God. In this chapter we will look at some biblical principles about receiving the Spirit's empowering.

1. EMPOWERING IS AN EXPERIENCE

As we have seen, the indwelling of the Spirit is usually not manifestly apparent to an outside observer. The new Christian doesn't necessarily feel anything when the Holy Spirit comes to live in his or her heart.

But the empowering of the Spirit is *experiential*. When the Spirit comes upon you, you *know* something has happened. His empowering is evident to you, and it is often evident to others around you.

When Philip preached in Samaria, many Samaritans were saved. It was obvious to Philip, however, that the Holy Spirit had not yet come upon any of them (see Acts 8:16). This indicates that there were *outward signs* Philip looked for to determine whether a person had received the Spirit's empowering.

When word arrived in Jerusalem that the Samaritans had been saved but not empowered, the Jerusalem church sent Peter and John to lay hands on the Samaritans. As Peter and John laid hands on these Samaritans, something happened! They had a definite and *observable* experience with the Spirit (see Acts 8:18,19).

What the Samaritans experienced was so dramatic, Simon the magician offered Peter and John money to teach him how to do the same. This passage doesn't say what the outward signs were, but they were impressive enough that a professional magician was willing to pay money to learn them! I've known some magicians and, believe me, they don't offer money for a trick unless it's impressive!

What these Samaritan Christians experienced, like my friend Ben and many others in the Bible, was a *power encounter* with the Spirit of God.

Many people get very uncomfortable when we talk about experiences with God. Some Christians are even taught to fear experiences. But it's not wrong to want to experience the One who loved you and gave His life for you. The men and women of the Bible did not hesitate to seek experiences with God.

David and the other psalmists *longed* to experience God's presence (see Pss. 42 and 61).

The Bible consistently teaches that the empowering of the Spirit is experiential. When the power and presence of the Holy Spirit are manifested in the life of a believer, discernible changes take place.

Sometimes the evidence of empowering is the release of a spiritual gift. As you read through the Bible, you find that the empowering of the Spirit is frequently accompanied by the person either speaking in tongues or prophesying (see Acts 2; 10:45,46; 19:5,6). This is still true today. If a person has not been taught against the modern validity of these gifts, the release of these gifts is a common response to the Spirit's empowering.

The Spirit also demonstrates His empowering presence in a number of other ways. Sometimes, as I pray for people to be empowered by the Spirit, there is the sensation of a mantle of heat coming down upon them. Sometimes they have felt overwhelmed by waves of power. There is occasionally an unexplainable weeping, trembling or even a violent shaking. Sometimes they simply fall over unconscious. Those are all biblical "calling cards" of the Spirit. They are His way of saying, "I'm here now to empower you."

While the evidence of the Spirit's presence may vary from one occasion to another, I believe the empowering is always experiential.

2. EMPOWERING IS SUDDEN

In His *indwelling* ministry, the Holy Spirit works to mature us through a gradual process. It takes time to form the character of Christ in us. (See 1 Pet. 3:18; Rom. 5:4.)

In His *empowering* ministry, God works through a sudden outpouring—a baptism, an inundation with His presence—to drench us with His power. If you've been to the ocean shore and have had a big wave roll in and crash down upon you, you know what it means to be inundated. That's the kind of language the Bible uses to describe empowering. It doesn't take a long time; it's just suddenly there.

That's why a very young Christian can sometimes exercise great power. A brand-new Christian who has received the Spirit's empowering may be able to receive words from the Lord, pray for the sick and see them healed, speak with other tongues or prophesy to reveal the secrets of men's hearts. These things are possible because the exercise of God's power is not dependent on growth. God's power is freely given to any of His children who truly desire and seek it.

One reason many Christians never experience God's power is that they never seek it! Some have been taught that it is wrong to seek God's power. They talk as though it would be presumptuous to ask God for it. This couldn't be further from the truth! In 1 Corinthians 12—14, we are told to earnestly desire the gifts and power of God. The apostle Paul did not hesitate to yearn for more of this power! He said that he suffered great hardships so that he could more fully know the power of His resurrection (see Phil. 3:10).

It is not "more spiritual" to live a powerless Christian life. God wants His people to have access to His power in order to walk in victory, and He is willing to pour His power out on all who will seek it.

3. EMPOWERING MUST BE MAINTAINED

It is important to remember that the empowering of the Spirit is not a once-and-for-all occurrence. After your initial inundation by the Spirit, you will need subsequent times of filling and additional anointings of the Spirit for specific purposes. We see that Peter and the other apostles were filled with God's power in Acts 2, but then they prayed again and were filled again in Acts 4.

The New Testament also seems to indicate there are different levels of empowering. Your initial empowering may not give you a great deal of power, but as you keep going back to God for more and faithfully use what He gives, you will increase your capacity to function in the power of God.

Don't be satisfied with your initial experience of empowering. Keep going back to the Lord and receiving more. His power is in infinite supply!

LIFESTYLES OF THE NEWLY EMPOWERED

When people receive the empowering of the Holy Spirit, it is natural that they will experience some very definite changes in their lives. Here are a few things to look for.

A NEW DESIRE FOR PRAISE AND WORSHIP

Be filled with the Spirit. Speak to one another with psalms, hymns and spiritual songs. Sing and make music in your heart to the Lord, always giving thanks to God the Father for everything, in the name of our Lord Jesus Christ (Eph. 5:18-20).

When the Holy Spirit invaded my life back in 1983, one of the first changes I noticed was the release of praise to God. As I mentioned in the introduction, I had been in a state of deep depression when, in response to prayer, the Holy Spirit invaded our house overnight. When I awoke the next morning, praise songs were filling my mind.

All through the day, there was a constant flow of praise to Jesus, almost like "background music." Song bubbled up from my spirit with no conscious effort on my part. There was a a a richness, satisfaction and joy in praising Jesus unlike anything I had ever felt. As I drifted off to sleep that night, my spirit was still overflowing with praise.

In the weeks that followed, I picked up the guitar I hadn't played in years and God began to give me new songs. Sometimes I would be reading a passage of Scripture, and I would hear a tune that went with it. I would sit with Him for hours, singing songs of love and praise to Jesus. This went on for months.

Not everyone has that experience when the Spirit comes upon them, but it's not unusual. Ephesians 5 says to be filled with the Spirit, singing to one another in psalms.

The empowering of the Holy Spirit releases a river of praise in our spirits. That's why charismatic and Pentecostal churches usually put such a strong emphasis on praise and worship. Before our church was invaded by the Spirit, we were satisfied with two or three hymns on Sunday morning, and most people seemed impatient with *that*. Now we have over an hour of praise and worship every Sunday and nobody wants to stop! The presence of the Spirit gives us a desire for intimacy with God that can only be satisfied in praise and worship.

SUPERNATURAL MANIFESTATIONS

Frequently when a person is empowered by the Spirit, he or she will experience the release of tongues or prophecy. These two manifestations of the Spirit are just the starting point, however. I believe once someone is filled with the Holy Spirit, he or she has the capacity to function in any of the gifts of the Spirit described in 1 Corinthians 12. We will study more about the gifts of the Spirit in a later chapter.

SPIRITUAL DISCERNMENT
When you are empowered by the Spirit, you also gain discernment and perception of the spiritual realm. Many testify that when they are filled with the Spirit, they feel like a blind man whose eyes have just been opened. They are suddenly aware of a previously unseen level of spiritual reality.

A NEW LEVEL OF WARFARE
When you are empowered by the Spirit, you become much more of a threat to Satan's kingdom, and consequently you find yourself catapulted into a new level of warfare. My friend John Dickson says the real sign of the baptism of the Holy Spirit is not tongues, but *trouble*. That's because most people experience an increased level of spiritual attack for several months after the Spirit's filling.

This season of spiritual attack lasts until we recognize what it is and learn to put on our spiritual armor as described in Ephesians 6. By way of encouragement, we should note that it is not God's will for you to walk through this period in defeat, under the oppression of the enemy (see Rom. 8:31-35). He has provided all you need to walk in continual triumph, but you do need to take His provision seriously!

EQUIPPING FOR MINISTRY

You will receive power when the Holy Spirit comes on you; and you will be my witnesses . . . to the ends of the earth (Acts 1:8).

The whole purpose of the Spirit's empowering is to equip you to minister to others, to change individual lives through the power of God and to disciple the nations.

The Lord promises in Acts 1:8, "You will receive power...*and you will be my witnesses*" (italics mine). If all we were to do was sit in church and sing some nice songs, we wouldn't need empowering. But God has given us a job to do. We have a world to win! We have territory to take back from the enemy. There are lives to be set free from Satan's bondage. And to do that we need His power.

QUENCHING THE SPIRIT

It is possible to be a mature Christian, to allow the indwelling Spirit to produce His character in your life, and yet know very little of His power. This was true of the church at Thessalonica.

In his first letter to the Thessalonians, Paul complimented them on their maturity and their walk with the Lord. He also expressed a concern, however, warning them, "Do not put out the Spirit's fire; do not treat prophecies with contempt. Test everything. Hold on to the good" (1 Thess. 5:19-21).

God doesn't want you to choose between maturity and power. He wants you to have both.

The Thessalonians knew the Spirit's indwelling and were well on their way to becoming mature Christians. The character of Jesus was being formed in them. But the display of the Spirit's power made them uncomfortable.

They saw that when the Holy Spirit began working in power there was often some confusion. (It takes time for people to learn to function in God's gifts with maturity.) The Thessalonians wanted to take the easy way out. They wanted to forbid prophecy and focus on the more "orderly" and "acceptable" activities of learning the Word and growing to maturity. Paul warned them not to grieve the Spirit by rejecting His manifestations.

God doesn't want you to choose between maturity and power. He wants you to have both. He wants you to repent, submit and feed on the Word. He wants you to grow to maturity, but He also wants to equip you to function effectively in His power.

RECEIVING HIS POWER

While many Christians agree that it is important to be empowered by the Holy Spirit, there is a great diversity of opinion on how to receive that power.

Some are empowered without seeking it. When I was "baptized" in the Spirit's power, I had not sought it. I wasn't even sure I wanted it. I received it by the sovereign grace of God. Something similar happened in the New Testament with Cornelius. Cornelius and his friends were not seeking an experience with the Spirit; they just wanted to know the Lord. But as Peter presented the gospel and faith stirred in their hearts, the Spirit of God fell upon them in power and they spoke with other tongues, just as the apostles did at Pentecost (see Acts 10:44-46).

While there are some today who experience the Spirit's power without seeking it, the Bible makes it clear that these are the exceptions. In most cases the empowering of the Spirit must be sought. God wants us to desire His Spirit and pray for His fullness.

Different groups have taken different approaches to seeking the Spirit's power. Dr. Garnet Pike, a Pentecostal theologian, wrote one of the best books ever written on receiving the power of the Holy Spirit. In this book, *Receiving the Promise of the*

Father, Dr. Pike describes how different groups attempt to bring men and women into the empowering experience.

Dr. Pike characterizes the approach of classical Pentecostalism as "tarrying" for the Spirit's power. In this method, the individual seeking "the baptism" is surrounded by a group of people who are loudly praying in tongues and praising God, usually accompanied by loud music. Emotions are stirred and much zeal is evident. In many cases, however, there is little understanding, and many go away discouraged.

In contrast to this, Dr. Pike describes an approach, typical of many in the charismatic movement, involving "teaching" the seeker to speak in tongues. This is sometimes accomplished by having the seeker repeat a phrase over and over while others cluster around and pray in tongues. "Sometimes unique expressions that sounded like 'shondalai' or 'look at my tie' or 'should have bought a Honda!' were spoken," Dr. Pike writes. "The speaking pace was quickened until the counselor would say, 'You got it!'"[1]

Then there is the approach often used in the Vineyard and "Third Wave" churches. In the Third Wave approach, the Spirit's power is received by standing or sitting very still while someone prays, "Come, Holy Spirit."

In recent years much of the Church has experienced some version of the Toronto Blessing-style of renewal. In these services the key is laying on the floor—doing "carpet time"—long enough to "soak" in the power of the Spirit.

While some of these methods seem strange, the fact is that many godly believers have had life-changing experiences with the Spirit in each of these ways. That's because the issue in receiving God's power is not the outward form, method or style of ministry, but a heart that yearns after the Lord and is hungry to receive His power. If you have such a heart and seek His power persistently, you will experience the Spirit's empowering. But be willing to receive it in any way He desires to impart it!

KEYS TO RECEIVING

While the Bible never gives a formula for receiving the Spirit's power, a study of the Word reveals two key elements that are frequently present. The first of these is the *prayer of faith*.

EMPOWERED THROUGH PRAYER

The first and most crucial step toward being empowered is *prayer*. In Luke 11:13, Jesus speaks of the empowering ministry of the Spirit and tells us that the Father gives the Spirit to those who ask.

In the book of Acts, we find the apostles "joined together constantly in prayer" (Acts 1:14). The result was "they were all filled with the Holy Spirit" (Acts 2:4, *NKJV*).

Later, we read that the disciples "raised their voices together in prayer to God" (Acts 4:24). Again the result was "they were all filled with the Holy Spirit" (Acts 4:31).

The prayer that releases the Spirit's power is not just a repetition of words, but a conscious expression of faith in God's willingness and desire to give you His power (see Gal. 3:5). One expression of this faith is the willingness to persevere, to continue seeking until you have received (see Luke 11:5-13). Like my friend Ben, many are not filled the first time they ask, but if they keep seeking they will receive.

EMPOWERED THROUGH IMPARTATION

The second key to receiving the Spirit's power is *impartation*, usually through the laying on of hands. The Spirit's power *can* come directly from God in response to prayer, but on most occasions God chooses to give or *impart* His power through another believer.

Remember the apostle Paul's dramatic conversion experience on the Damascus road when he encountered the glorified

Jesus? Although Paul's conversion was dramatic, he was not empowered by the Holy Spirit until another believer, Ananias, came and laid hands on him, praying for the Spirit to fill him. The Word consistently shows the power of the Spirit being imparted in this way. (See Acts 8:14-17 and Acts 9:11-17 for two examples.)

This pattern holds true today. God gives His people the privilege of imparting the fullness of His Spirit by the laying on of hands. Hebrews 6 identifies the laying on of hands as one of the six foundational principles of the Christian life.

Why does God choose to work through the laying on of human hands? Why does He not just release His anointing directly to each believer? I believe God imparts His power from one believer to another in this way to demonstrate the need for *unity* in the Body of Christ. God does not want us to be "Lone Ranger" Christians. We need each other, and He wants us to recognize that need.

If you are seeking to receive the Spirit's power, what then must you do? The first step is to seek the Lord. Tell him you desire His power, and ask Him to baptize you in the power of the Holy Spirit.

The next step is to seek out a trusted Christian friend or pastor who is filled with the Spirit and have him or her pray over you to impart the Spirit's power.

If you have done this and nothing has yet happened, keep seeking (see Matt. 7:9). The things we really want from God we must be willing to ask for again and again. Perseverance is a sign of faith (see 1 Tim. 4:16; Heb. 12:1).

As you continue to pray, spend time in the Word to increase your understanding of the Holy Spirit and His work. As you do this, spiritual hindrances will be removed, and you will find yourself able to freely receive the Spirit's power.

IMPARTING THE FULLNESS
OF THE SPIRIT

One of the most exciting privileges I have in ministry is imparting to another believer the empowering of the Holy Spirit, an event that will immediately and profoundly change that believer's life. Here are some suggestions for leading a person to receive the empowering of the Holy Spirit:

1. Teach him or her what the Bible says about this experience. It is good to begin with a solid biblical understanding of this ministry of the Spirit. It is also important for the Christian to be committed to growing to maturity through the Spirit's indwelling ministry.

2. Have him pray and ask God for the empowering of the Spirit. (You will sometimes be led to have him confess any known sins to God. This is not always necessary, but it's always a good idea!)

3. Lay your hand gently on his head and invite the Holy Spirit to come upon him and empower him.

4 Have him relax and wait upon the Lord. Follow the instructions in the last chapter of this book. Assure the believer that God will answer his prayer. Instruct him to simply receive what God is doing. (Don't let him get too tense. When a person tenses up, he is less sensitive to what the Spirit is trying to do.)

5. When you sense the Spirit upon him, you may be led to pray for God to release His gifts to the person. Often at this point, there is some involuntary movement of the throat, lips or tongue. This can be an indication that the Spirit is releasing the gift of tongues to the person. If this happens, encourage him to express the gift of tongues, but don't make an issue of it.

6. If not much happens, don't make the person feel

guilty. This might not be the time God has for him, or there may be some blockage there you are not aware of. Encourage him to continue seeking His power. Encourage the person to study through the book of Acts and see what it says about the Holy Spirit. Volunteer to pray with him again at another time. God promises if they keep seeking, they *will* find.

7. If the Spirit touches the person, rejoice with him. Thank God together for the Spirit's empowering work. Encourage him to study through the book of Acts and 1 Corinthians 12—14. Encourage the person to regularly meet with other Christians to learn how to use the gifts of the Spirit in a mature and edifying way (see Acts 2:46,47).

MINISTRY IN THE SPIRIT: DOING THE WORK OF THE KINGDOM

Even before the doorbell rang, we knew Pat would come. Our seven-year-old daughter had been feeling poorly for several days, and by that afternoon she had developed a full-blown sinus infection. Earlier in the morning, as her symptoms grew worse, our daughter observed, "Well, I'm sick again! I guess it's time for Pat to come!"

Sure enough, when Linda answered the door, there was Pat.

Pat was our "charismatic friend." We had known Pat for several years, and we knew she had a relationship with the Holy Spirit we didn't understand. We might not see Pat for six months, but if one of the kids got sick, Pat would always call or come by.

As Linda opened the door, I heard Pat's usual cheerful greeting. "Hello! The Lord just put you guys on my heart this morning, so I thought I'd drop by and see if anyone here needs prayer."

Pat's routine was always the same. She would come in, express her sympathy for whoever was sick, pray in tongues (which we didn't believe in) and pray for God to heal the sick family member (which we also didn't believe in). We knew exactly what to expect, because Pat had come by like this at least twenty times in the last four years.

At first we hadn't thought much about it. Pat was a nice lady who really loved the Lord, so we humored her strange charismatic beliefs and allowed her to come and pray. It wasn't long, though, before a definite pattern emerged. Every time Pat came and prayed, healing took place. Usually within two or three hours there would be definite improvement, and by the next morning the sickness would be totally gone!

This experience totally contradicted the theology I had been taught in seminary. Yet as Pat came and ministered to us time and again, God worked through her to do a major work in our lives.

Pat was not a professional minister. She was not on a church staff. She didn't have it all together. She had problems in her life, just like everybody else. But she had learned how to pray for sick people. And God worked through her to change our lives.

WHO IS A MINISTER?

As we have seen, the power of the Holy Spirit is available to every true Christian. God desires to empower *you*, and He has a purpose for this empowering. The Lord doesn't fill you so you can sit around and *feel* empowered. He wants to equip you to minister (see 1 Tim. 4:6). So what does it mean to minister in the power of the Spirit?

In Paul's letter to the Ephesians, we find a revolutionary statement:

It was [Jesus] who gave some to be apostles, some to be prophets, some to be evangelists, and some to be pastors and teachers, to prepare God's people for works of service, so that the body of Christ may be built up (Eph. 4:11,12).

The *New King James Version* says He established these roles "for the equipping of the saints for the work of ministry."

That statement turned my understanding of "church" upside down! Like most Christians, I was raised to think of ministry as the work of the pastor. I thought that to be "in the ministry" you must attend seminary and find a church to pastor.

In this passage, Paul completely reverses that way of thinking. He tells us *it is not the job of the pastor to do the work of ministry!* The work of the ministry is the job of "God's people," and that includes all of us—every Christian. If you are a Christian, God has called you to minister!

If it's the job of every Christian to minister, what's the *pastor* supposed to do? Paul explains that, too. The job of church leaders—including apostles, prophets, evangelists, pastors and teachers—is to *equip* the saints. The leaders of the church are to act as trainers or coaches, equipping the saints to do the works of Jesus.

This is not a common understanding in the Church today, but that's how the Early Church functioned. Let's look for a moment at Acts 2.

When the day of Pentecost came, Jerusalem was filled with men and women from all over the Roman Empire. These people had made the pilgrimage to Jerusalem to celebrate the Jewish feast. They were not professional ministers. They were not graduates of rabbinical schools or seminaries; these were ordinary people. They were farmers, businessmen, fishermen, carpenters and homemakers. They represented a cross section of first-century Judaism.

Then, the Holy Spirit fell. These average, ordinary people heard the sound of rushing wind and witnessed the apostles speaking in other languages. They were perplexed. When they crowded around to get a better look, Peter stood up and began to speak. As they heard Peter's sermon, they were pierced to the heart and gave their lives to Jesus. Three thousand ordinary men and women were now brand-new Christians.

Following their conversion, these people stayed in Jerusalem, devoting themselves to the apostles' teaching, fellowship, breaking of bread and prayer (see Acts 2:42).

Let's skip ahead a few years to the events of Acts 8. The Church had grown to the point that the leaders of Judaism were feeling threatened. Persecution broke out, beginning with the martyrdom of Stephen.

In response to this persecution, the believers headed for the hills! Thousands of Christians went out from Jerusalem. "On that day a great persecution broke out against the church at Jerusalem, and *all except the apostles* were scattered throughout Judea and Samaria" (Acts 8:1, italics mine).

Who was it that went out into Judea and Samaria? Everyone in the Church—except the apostles. The apostles stayed in Jerusalem, and the ordinary "laymen" left. But notice what happens: "Those who had been scattered preached the word wherever they went" (Acts 8:4).

These people were not the Church's leadership. These were the same average, ordinary people who got saved back in chapter 2. But, just a few years later, they were all out preaching!

What was their ministry like?

Philip went down to a city in Samaria and proclaimed the Christ there. When the crowds heard Philip and saw the miraculous signs he did, they all paid close attention to what he said. With shrieks, evil spirits came out of many, and many paralytics and cripples were healed. So there was great joy in that city (Acts 8:5-8).

The structure of the biblical passage from which this account is taken indicates Philip's ministry was more or less typical of what these Christians did. He wasn't the pastor of a church. He wasn't a prophet. His job in the church had been to wait on tables! (See Acts 6:1-5.)

But Philip went out and performed miracles. He healed the sick, cast out demons and led many to the Lord. First Corinthians 12 tells us that healings, miracles and prophetic words were common to the ministry of ordinary Christians in the Early Church. As a result, in a very short time the Church had spread and prospered all through the region.

In Acts 2 we saw a small group of apostles ministering to thousands of brand-new Christians. In Acts 8 we see those thousands of Christians doing the work of ministry while the apostles stayed home.

What do you suppose the apostles had been doing with these people in the years between Acts 2 and Acts 8? They had been equipping the saints for the work of ministry! They had taught them to preach the gospel, to cast out demons, to heal the sick and to do everything Jesus had taught His disciples to do.

In the Early Church, the leaders did not function as the ministers while the laypersons sat and watched. The leaders taught the *laity* to minister. The result was incredible church growth.

Suppose the twelve apostles had gone out into Judea and Samaria themselves the day after Pentecost. What would have happened? There would have been only twelve people doing the work of ministry, and their work would have had a limited impact.

But instead of heading out to Judea and Samaria, the apostles stayed with the converts in Jerusalem and trained them. The fruit of their labors was *thousands* of trained ministers who went out and tremendously affected the entire region.

That's still God's plan for ministry. He doesn't want ministry to be limited to pastors and church leaders. Some of the most effective ministry is done by ordinary Christians who are trained and equipped to minister—people like our friend Pat.

All of His people are to be involved in winning the lost, making disciples, healing the sick, comforting the brokenhearted and manifesting His love to a hurting world. In our church, we've heard incredible testimonies of God's power at work through ordinary people.

Real Life Testimony

Five years ago, our brother Paul was digging a hole in his backyard when he ruptured two discs in his back. For years afterward he was pretty much in constant pain.

One evening recently, at a home group meeting, John asked if he could pray for Paul. John, who works in the personnel department in a large manufacturing firm, lightly touched Paul's outstretched hands and prayed for the power of the Holy Spirit to be released into Paul. Immediately, Paul fell to the floor. He lay there, rolling back and forth, appearing to wrestle with an unseen force for about twenty minutes. At the end of that time he heard the Lord say, "You're free."

Paul got up from the floor, completely free of pain! Days passed and the pain did not return. Paul, determined to test what appeared to be a supernatural healing, went into his backyard and dug a hole three feet wide and three feet deep, and then proceeded to fill the hole back in—all with absolutely no pain! The Spirit of God had worked through John to perform a miraculous healing.

I was personally present when this healing took place and have known the people involved for a number of years. I can testify that it took place just as described.

Jesus promised that those who believe in Him would do the same works He did. Through the power of the Spirit that promise is being fulfilled.

WHAT IS MINISTRY?

If God has called us to the work of ministry, it's imperative that we understand what ministry is. I like to define ministry in terms of two kingdoms—the *kingdom of God* and the *kingdom of this world.*

When most of us hear the word "kingdom," we think of a geographical territory. The Bible, however, describes "kingdom," not in terms of territory, but in terms of *will* and *rule.* Jesus taught the disciples to pray, "May your kingdom come, may your will be done on earth as it is in heaven" (Matt. 6:10, *TEV*). Where God's *will* is done, there His *kingdom* is manifested.

Originally there was only one kingdom in the universe, the kingdom of God. Yahweh ruled as King, and His will was perfectly accomplished throughout His creation. When Satan rebelled against the Lord, a second will was introduced (see Ezek. 28:12-19; Isa. 14:12-15). Satan drew away one-third of the angels and established a rebel kingdom to oppose God's purposes.

Where Satan's will is done, Satan's kingdom is manifested. Some people are offended by the suggestion that God's will is not being perfectly accomplished on the earth. They assume everything that happens must be God's will. When tragedy strikes, they say, "It must be the will of God."

The Bible assures us that everything that happens is *not* God's will! Jesus would not have told us to pray for God's will to be done if it was already being done. God's Word tells us this world is presently controlled by Satan and his forces. Satan is the ruler of this world (see Eph. 2:2) and the god of this age (see 2 Cor. 4:4). First John 5:19 says, "The whole world is under the control of the evil one."

When Jesus came to this world, He came as an invader to reestablish the rule of God on this planet. He announced that, through His coming, the kingdom of God was at hand (see Matt. 4:17). At the second coming, Jesus will one day destroy Satan's kingdom and fully establish His rule on the earth. During the present age, however, these two kingdoms exist side by side. They are kingdoms in conflict: the kingdom of God versus the kingdom of this world.

If we are to understand ministry, it is vital that we recognize which kingdom is being manifested in any given situation. The Bible teaches that Satan is an evil tyrant whose purpose is to steal, kill and destroy (see John 10:10). Satan's will is to oppress and torment those who are under his dominion and to bring destruction to everything that is God's. Wherever you see sin, hatred, oppression, poverty, sickness or suffering, there *Satan's* kingdom is being manifested.

Healing and deliverance—ministries of the Holy Spirit—tear down the works of the enemy and manifest God's kingdom in the lives of the people.

The sign that God's kingdom is present is that *His* good will is being done. How do we know when the will of God is being perfectly accomplished? One way to know is to look at the biblical descriptions of heaven. In heaven, God's will is *always* perfectly accomplished.

What is heaven like? The Bible reveals that in heaven there is no sin, no hunger, no pain, no sickness and no suffering. In the one place where God's will is always perfectly accomplished, we find fullness of joy, fullness of provision, perfect righteousness and perfect health.

Jesus says we should pray that God's will be accomplished on earth as it is in heaven (see Matt. 6:9,10). When that is accomplished—when the righteousness, health, peace and joy that characterize heaven are manifested on earth—God's kingdom has been manifested.

We see that in the Gospels. Jesus announced that, when He healed the sick and cast out demons, the kingdom of God had indeed "come upon" the earth (Matt. 12:28). Healing and deliverance were means of bringing situations on earth into line with the will of God. These ministries tear down the works of the enemy and manifest God's kingdom in the lives of people.

CHARACTERISTICS OF THE KINGDOMS

Let us look at some of the specific traits that characterize these two kingdoms. Because of Satan's cruel domination, his kingdom is characterized by...

People who are separated from God
People who are enslaved to sin
People who are oppressed by the enemy
People with broken relationships
People with physical sickness and pain
People who are hungry and in need
People who are sorrowful and in distress
People who are brokenhearted and in despair

These are the characteristics of the realm of darkness. They are the works of the evil one. Wherever Satan has had his way, such things are evident.

The kingdom of God is also characterized by certain traits. Where God's kingdom is manifested, we find...

People who have been reconciled to God
People living a holy life with sins forgiven
People set free from the oppression of the enemy
People restored in their relationships
People living in physical health
People whose needs are met with God's
abundant provision
Peace and joy in the Holy Spirit
People with hearts of praise to God

These are the characteristics of the realm of light. These things are the will of GOD. You will find these things wherever God's will is perfectly manifested. When we get to heaven, all these will be true—all the time!

If we understand the difference between these two kingdoms, we can begin to understand what ministry is.

Ministry is the process of...

...rescuing men and women out of the kingdom of darkness

...and bringing them into the kingdom of light.

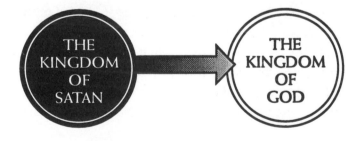

...setting men and women free from captivity to Satan

...and bringing their lives into line with the perfect will of God.

...delivering men and women from sin and its effects

...so they can experience the fullness of God's blessing.

John Wimber described ministry this way:

We are thrust into the middle of a battle with Satan: it's a tug-of-war and the prize is the souls of men and women. Satan's captivity of men and women has many facets, but denying them final salvation is his primary goal. But there are other types of dominion: bondage to sin, physical and emotional problems, social disruption and demonic affliction. Our mission is to rescue those who have been taken captive as a result of Adam's fall.[1]

The process of ministry takes many forms:

Ministry is finding people who are *separated* from God and *reconciling* them to God.

It is finding people *enslaved to sin* and leading them into a *holy life* where they can walk in God's forgiveness.

It is finding people *oppressed* by the enemy and setting them *free*.

It is finding people with *broken relationships* and helping those relationships be *restored*.

It is finding people with physical *sickness* and pain and bringing them *healing*.

It is finding people who are *hungry and in need* and meeting those needs with *God's abundant provision*.

It is finding people who are *sorrowful and in distress* and filling them with *peace and joy in the Holy Spirit*.

It is finding people who are *brokenhearted and in despair* and giving them *hearts of praise to God*.

When Jesus described His ministry in Luke 4:18, He quoted Isaiah 61:1-3. In this passage, the prophet Isaiah foretells the ministry of Jesus and describes it in similar terms:

The Spirit of the Sovereign Lord is on me, because the Lord has anointed me to preach good news to the poor. He has sent me to bind up the brokenhearted, to proclaim freedom for the captives and release from darkness for the prisoners, to proclaim the year of the Lord's favor and the day of vengeance of our God, to comfort all who mourn, and provide for those who grieve in Zion—to bestow on them a crown of beauty instead of ashes, the oil of gladness instead of mourning, and a garment of praise instead of a spirit of despair. They will be called oaks of righteousness, a planting of the Lord for the display of his splendor.

Throughout Jesus' ministry, His work was to deliver men and women out of darkness into light, manifesting the kingdom of God at the point of need in their lives. That is the work of ministry.

WALKING IN THE ANOINTING

Mac and I entered the hospital room with more than a little trepi-
dation. The woman in the bed had been having severe headaches
and the preliminary diagnosis was a brain tumor. She did not go to
our church; in fact, we had never seen her before, but a mutual
friend had asked us to pray for her.

The woman appeared to be in her early fifties, and was obviously
in a lot of pain. Nevertheless she seemed genuinely happy to see us.
When we introduced ourselves, she assured us she knew Jesus and
yes, she would like very much for us to pray for her.

The woman's teenage daughter sat in a chair at the far end of
the room, chain-smoking and eyeing us with suspicion. We could
tell she had been crying, and she was clearly very upset about her
mother's condition.

As I laid my hand gently on the woman's head, I prayed a
simple prayer asking for the Holy Spirit to come and minister to
her. Immediately the Spirit fell on her with great power. She began
to breathe very deeply and her whole body started to shake and
tremble.

That really got the daughter's attention. She stood up and took
a few steps closer to the bed to get a better look at what was
happening to her mother. Responding to a prompting from the

Spirit, Mac turned to the daughter and said, "Come over here. I think God wants you to pray for your mother."

The daughter immediately took a step back. "I...I can't!" she stammered in fear. "I don't know Jesus!"

"Well, let me introduce you to Jesus and then you can pray for her," Mac responded. The girl was willing, so Mac quickly led her through a two-minute presentation of the gospel and the sinner's prayer. With tears streaming down her face the girl invited Jesus into her heart, then came over and prayed for her mother's healing.

After about five more minutes, the mother relaxed, and a look of peace came over her face. The headache was gone and did not return.

Further medical tests failed to find any medical problem, and after a few days of observation, the woman was released to go home.

The above story actually happened. A mother was healed and a daughter was saved because of a demonstration of God's power. God doesn't want this kind of occurrence to be an unusual event. He wants His children to be equipped to minister in such supernatural power that lives are changed and His kingdom manifested on earth.

THE SOURCE OF MINISTRY

Isaiah 61 not only describes the work of ministry, but it also gives the source of ministry. Isaiah 61:1 begins, "The Spirit of the Sovereign Lord is on me, because the Lord has *anointed* me."

God tells us that the source of Jesus' ministry was the *anointing* of the Holy Spirit. Jesus ministered by releasing the *anointing*—the power of the Spirit—to meet needs and change situations. According to the Scriptures, Jesus didn't perform any works of ministry until the power of the Spirit came upon

Him (see Mark 1:10). There is no record He did even one act of ministry before that time!

I believe He did that as an example for his followers, to demonstrate that we cannot minister in human power. If Jesus, the sinless Son of God, did not try to minister without the anointing of the Holy Spirit, neither should we.

One of the most important things we can understand about ministry is that ministry deals with a commodity. That commodity is the anointing of God. Without anointing, there is no ministry.

If a painter wants to paint a picture, she needs paint.

If a cook wants to prepare a meal, he needs the proper ingredients.

If a Christian wants to minister, that Christian needs the anointing of the Holy Spirit.

If you want to do the work of ministry, the anointing is not optional. Your highest priority is to receive and maintain the power of God in your life.

WHAT IS THE ANOINTING?

When we hear the word "anointing," we sometimes think of the biblical practice of pouring a little olive oil on a person's head. The act of anointing with oil is not just a religious ritual, but a symbolic act that releases a deeper reality. When we, in faith, anoint someone with oil, we are asking the Holy Spirit to pour out His supernatural power, or *dunamis*, to heal or equip that person for service.

The real issue in anointing is the power of God. Jesus was the *Messiah*, or "Anointed One," not because He had oil on His head, but because He walked in the *power* of the Holy Spirit. We can pour oil on a person's head, but only the Holy Spirit can pour out the power of God. When you are filled with the Holy Spirit, you receive an enduement of power. That power is the *anointing* of God.

The Bible describes God's anointing as a *tangible* substance. Not just a spiritual transaction to be taken by faith, the anointing is substantial and real, its presence discernible by our human senses. In Mark 5, when the woman touched the fringe of His garment, Jesus *felt* the power of God go out from Him to heal.

Many times as you pray for the sick you will feel a strong sensation of heat or tingling in your hands. That's the power, the anointing of God flowing out to accomplish God's purposes.

Anointing is not only tangible, it's *transferable*. It flows like water. It is conducted like electricity. It is transferred from one person to another by physical touch. Notice how the anointing is described in the following passages:

> People brought all their sick to him and begged him to let the sick just touch the edge of his cloak, and all who touched him were healed (Matt. 14:35,36).

> The people all tried to touch him, because power was coming from him and healing them all (Luke 6:19).

> She came up behind him in the crowd and touched his cloak, because she thought, "If I just touch his clothes, I will be healed." Immediately her bleeding stopped and she felt in her body that she was freed from her suffering (Mark 5:27-29).

That's the anointing of God. The person receiving ministry frequently feels the anointing as it performs its work in his or her body.

Kenneth Hagin describes the dramatic account of an alcoholic set free by the anointing of God. This man had been an officer in the U.S. Army, but had become a hopeless alcoholic. By the age of 60, he had spent time in six different hospitals, gone through the treatment programs, and came out drinking just as much as when he went in. Finally, in desperation, he came to a Kenneth Hagin meeting to receive ministry.

When Hagin laid hands on him, the man later reported, "Something like electricity went all over me—warmth went all over me!" The power was so great that he fell to the ground. The result was that he not only drew closer to the Lord, but was *instantly* delivered from alcoholism. He later testified that from that moment on he totally lost his craving for alcohol. He never even *wanted* another drink.[1]

The anointing of God can also temporarily rest on an inanimate object. There was enough anointing left in Elisha's dead bones to raise a man from the dead! (See 2 Kings 13:21.) Acts 19:12 describes the anointing of God being transferred from Paul to a piece of cloth, so that those who touched the cloth were healed! (I've heard many people ridicule the Pentecostal practice of using a prayer cloth. The book of Acts clearly demonstrates, however, that prayer cloths are biblical.) If such a transference of God's power seems strange to us, it's only an indication that we have lived with powerlessness so long we no longer understand how God's anointing operates.

When you are empowered by the Spirit, God places the anointing within you. If you are filled with the Holy Spirit, that anointing is there, *right now*, ready to flow out to accomplish God's purposes in the world.

Real Life Testimony

I was teaching a two-week pastoral training seminar to a group of Russian and Ukrainian pastors in a city near Odessa in Ukraine. In one of the evening sessions, I was explaining how to recognize when the Holy Spirit has come upon someone.

Seeking an example to use as a demonstration for ministry, I prayed and asked the Spirit of God to come. Almost immediately, the Holy Spirit fell in power on Lena, my interpreter. Out of habit, I reached out my hand, touched her lightly on the forehead and began to pray for her. Without warning, she collapsed on the floor, unconscious—and I was left standing in front of a group of Russian-speaking pastors without an interpreter!

I knelt down and prayed for Lena for a few minutes, and the Lord told me He was healing her. It was clear, however, she would not be doing any more interpreting that evening! Fortunately, there was another man there who knew some English and, with his help, we made it through the seminar. Lena finally got up after about twenty minutes, having had a wonderful time with the Lord.

On my next trip to Russia, Lena told me the rest of the story. She had had a congenital heart condition that had given her a lot of problems over the years. While she was on the floor under the anointing of the Holy Spirit, God had spoken to her and told her He was healing her, so she made an appointment with the doctor for a checkup. A few weeks later, when the doctor finished the examination, he informed her there was no longer any trace of a heart condition!

MAINTAINING THE ANOINTING

As you minister in the anointing of God, the power of the Holy Spirit will go out from you to accomplish the work of ministry. When the woman with the hemorrhage touched the hem of His garment, Jesus *felt the power go out from Him.*

Many times when you pray for the sick you will feel that

same sensation as God's anointing flows through your hands. As the anointing of God flows out from you, your supply of power is depleted. Many times after an evening of intense ministry, you will feel completely drained. The power is gone. You have nothing left to give.

If you are going to do the work of ministry, it is crucial that you learn how to restore and maintain the anointing. The Bible teaches that power for ministry is maintained through fellowship with God. The secret of maintaining the anointing is to constantly go back to the source. You go back to God and receive more.

Mark 1 describes a very busy day in the life of Jesus. He began at the synagogue where He preached and cast out a demon. Then He went to Peter's house and healed Peter's mother-in-law. That evening, the whole town came to Him, and He spent the evening healing and casting out demons. I imagine by the end of that time, He was exhausted. He was spiritually and physically drained. So what did He do? "Very early in the morning, while it was still dark, Jesus got up, left the house and went off to a solitary place, where he prayed" (Mark 1:35).

After such a busy day of ministry, most of us would have to sleep in the next morning, but Jesus got up before dawn and went out to spend time with the Father. That was often Jesus' response after an unusually intense time of ministry. In Mark 6:34-44, Jesus spent an entire day teaching the multitudes and healing the sick. He ended the day by feeding the 5,000.

After this eventful day, what did He do?

Jesus made his disciples get into the boat and go on ahead of him to Bethsaida, while he dismissed the crowd. After leaving them, he went up on a mountainside to pray (Mark 6:45,46).

Jesus sent the disciples away and spent most of the night in prayer. When He was weak, when He had given His all to the crowds, Jesus knew it was an absolute *necessity* to go back to the source and spend time in fellowship with the Father.

I believe this reveals a fundamental spiritual principle: *Spiritual power is an outflow of communion with God.*

When you are empowered by the Spirit, the power is not permanent. You need to constantly go back to the source for more. In Ephesians 5:18 the Greek text literally says "Be continually *being filled* with the Spirit" (italics mine). It describes a continual or a repeated action.

Get alone with God every day. Relax and allow His Spirit to minister to you and refresh you with His awesome power.

Remember, the same apostles who were filled with the Spirit in Acts 2 prayed and were filled again in Acts 4. If even the apostles needed a "refill," it is not surprising we frequently need one also. We need to spend time in the presence of God, in fellowship with Him, to restore our strength.

I would encourage you to get alone with God every day, and invite His Spirit to come and fill you. Relax and allow His Spirit to minister to you and refresh you with His awesome power.

RELEASING THE ANOINTING

How do you release the anointing of God to operate in a specific situation? The Bible tells us that the anointing is released by only one thing: *faith*. If there is no faith present, the anointing cannot flow. Even Jesus himself could do very little ministry in an atmosphere of general unbelief (see Matt. 13:58; Mark 6:5,6).

To learn to operate in the anointing is to learn to walk in faith. There are three things that can aid you as you learn to walk in the faith that releases anointing:

Knowledge of the Word. You can build your faith through study of the Bible. As you learn the promises of God and obey the instructions of His Word, your faith will grow. One of the study resources that has helped me learn to trust God in the area of healing is T. L. Osborn's classic book *Healing the Sick*. This book is so filled with Scripture about God's desire to heal that just reading it releases faith. Intellectual arguments that hinder faith cannot stand against the truth of God's Word.

Testimony of the Believers. Another way to build your faith is through hearing the testimonies of other Christians (see Rev. 12:11). This is just one reason why it's important to be part of a fellowship that not only believes in God's power but also exercises it. Surround yourself with people who operate in God's anointing. As you watch others minister in power and hear testimonies of what that power has accomplished, your faith will surely increase.

Real Life Testimony

My wife, Linda, had been suffering from an ovarian cyst for several weeks. The doctor had confirmed his diagnosis with a careful examination and a sonogram, and he offered little hope for a rapid recovery.

Although I had prayed for Linda several times, there was no noticeable improvement. As I left one evening to help minister at a city-wide revival meeting, I was in deep distress for her. She was doubled over in pain and could hardly walk. At the meeting, I prayed for several people and saw some of them dramatically healed. Yet, in my heart I was crying out to God to heal my wife.

When I arrived home that evening, Linda met me at the door, literally jumping up and down! "I'm healed!" she exclaimed, bubbling with excitement.

When I recovered from the shock, she told me the story. Shortly after I left for the meeting that evening, the Lord prompted Linda to call our old friend Pat and ask for prayer. As Pat prayed for her over the phone, Linda had a vision of Jesus and knew that if she could get to Him she would be healed. As she began to move toward Jesus, however, a dark shape rose up to block the way and obscure her vision. The dark shape hung before her for a few moments, but as Pat continued to pray, it suddenly rose up and flew out of sight. The vision ended, and the pain was gone!

When our doctor examined Linda again, there was not trace of the cyst. His comment was, "The only explanation I have is that you've been healed!"

The God who released His power to heal and perform miracles in biblical days has not changed. He is still a God who performs signs and wonders for those who will trust Him.

Personal Ministry Experience. A third way to build your faith is through personal experience in ministry. The more frequently you step out in obedience to minister and see God's power at work, the more your faith will increase.

THE OPPORTUNITY TO MINISTER

If you have been filled with the Spirit and desire to minister, where do you start? Where do you find *opportunities* to minister?

A study of the life of Jesus reveals three key principles for stepping out in ministry:

A. LOOK FOR PEOPLE IN NEED

We live in a world full of hurt and wounded people. They carry the scars of Satan's oppression on their bodies, minds and emotions. God is calling His people to minister in the power of the Holy Spirit, just as Jesus did, to bring healing to those oppressed by the devil (see Acts 10:38).

Jesus ministered to people at the point of their perceived need. A pressing need in a person's life is invariably an area where he or she is feeling the effects of living in the wrong kingdom—Satan's kingdom. These effects may include physical sickness, demonic oppression, guilt, anxiety, sorrow or perhaps an area of temptation the person cannot find the power to resist. Needs like these are all around us, and each one is an opportunity to minister.

Most ministry begins by reaching out to people you meet in the course of your normal daily activities: friends, coworkers, neighbors, relatives. That's what Jesus did. While at the synagogue, Jesus encountered a demonized man. His response was to minister to the need of that man, to set him free from the enemy's oppression (see Mark 1:23-26).

Jesus then went to Peter's house and found Peter's mother-in-law beset by illness. He went to her and ministered to her, and He healed her (see Mark 1:29-31).

That's how Jesus ministered. He never set up an artificial situation for ministry. He never went door to door. He never advertised a healing meeting in the *Jerusalem Daily News*. I'm not saying such methods are wrong, but Jesus didn't need to use them. He had a more effective way. During His three years of ministry, Jesus simply looked for people with needs. When He found a need, He met that need in the love and power of God.

That's the same way the Early Church ministered, and their evangelism efforts met with incredible success. Working in a hostile political climate under the constant threat of torture and death, they literally took the known world for Jesus in the span

---

When a life has been touched by God's supernatural power and provision, that person will be drawn to Him.

---

of about sixty years. And they did this without the benefit of radio, television, stadium conferences, mass mailings or any of the other modern methods of evangelism in use today. They would simply and without fanfare enter a city and see thousands of people come to Jesus!

What did they do to produce such results? Church historians tell us that one key to their incredible success was their ability to minister to people at the point of human need.

When you want to minister, begin to look for people with needs! It's not hard to find them. When you see a need, go and meet it. Simply say, "Can I help you?" or "Can I pray for you?" Pray for the person in need. Show him your love and concern. Go out of your way to meet his need (see Matt. 5:41). Allow the anointing of God to be released, so the person is healed, delivered or set free. When his life has been touched by God's supernatural power and provision, the person to whom you have ministered will be drawn to Him.

B. MINISTER TO THE PEOPLE GOD SENDS YOU

As you seek to minister to people in need, you will quickly

discover there are many more needs than you alone can meet. At that point you must exercise discernment as to *which* needs God wants *you* to minister to.

Even Jesus did not minister to everyone. When Jesus visited the pool of Bethesda, the courtyard was full of sick people. But He went to *one* person, healed him and then walked on (see John 5:1-15).

You might well ask, Why did He heal only one?

I believe He would answer, "I do only what I see the Father doing." Jesus did nothing on his own initiative. When He saw a need, He would ask the Father if this was a need *He* was to meet *right then.*

There were some needs God didn't want Jesus to meet. In Acts 3, we meet a lame beggar who sat at the Beautiful Gate of the Temple. Jesus probably walked past him many times. It was through this gate that Jesus entered the city during His triumphal entry. In all the times Jesus walked past this gate, He never healed the lame beggar. Why? I believe God was saving this man to be ministered to by Peter and John. God directed Peter and John to this man and he was healed. (See Acts 3:1-10.)

The Bible tells us God has prepared good works in advance for *you* to do (see Eph. 2:10). There are some needs God has specifically prepared you to meet. As you minister in these situations, you will find that great power is released. As you seek opportunities to minister, you will learn to develop a sensitivity to those needs the Holy Spirit has called you to meet.

At first, you will lack this sensitivity, and your ministry will not be as effective. That's okay. It takes time to learn. Just minister to as many as you can, and over the course of time you will gain this sensitivity.

C. WHEN YOUR MINISTRY IS EFFECTIVE, YOUR OPPORTUNITIES WILL MULTIPLY

When people see that you can minister effectively in a certain area, your opportunities for ministry will rapidly multiply. People will come to you.

That's what happened to Jesus. For example, when the people saw He was able to minister to a demonized man, they brought people to Him from all over the city (see Mark 1:32-34).

The first few times you pray for the sick, you may not see much happen. Your ability to exercise the gifts of the Spirit is dependent on your faith. But as you continue to pray for the sick, your faith will increase and you will see greater results more and more often. Then you won't need to worry about finding opportunities!

Begin to look for needs and meet them. The opportunities to minister will increase as your effectiveness increases.

THE MOTIVATION FOR MINISTRY

Jesus' motivation for ministry can be summed up in one word: *compassion*. He cared about people. Again and again in the Gospels we read that He had compassion on them and healed their sick (see Matt. 14:14). He had compassion on them and fed the hungry (see Matt. 15:32). He had compassion on them and opened their blind eyes (see Matt. 20:34). As He was filled with compassion, Jesus healed the sick, raised the dead, taught the multitudes and fed the hungry (see Luke 6:17-19, 7:14,15; Matt. 14:19-21).

He refused to do miracles just to show His power. When people came to Jesus and asked Him to show them a sign, He always declined (see Luke 23:8,9). His miracles were demonstrations of His love for people in need.

Jesus walked in compassion. After He healed all the sick in Capernaum, Jesus said to His disciples, "Let us go somewhere else—to the nearby villages—so I can preach there also. That is why I have come" (Mark 1:38).

Jesus was tired! He had had a busy day and a short night. He had been up since before dawn praying. But He was anxious to move on to the next place to minister, knowing there were many other people who needed Him. *His heart broke when He saw men and women oppressed by the enemy.*

The compassion of God will keep you going in ministry when you are fatigued. There will be evenings when you arrive home totally exhausted. You will want to fall into a chair and just relax for a while; but then someone calls with a need for ministry, so you get up and go. That's the love of God demonstrated.

Many times in ministry, your *love* will be just as important as the actual ministry you do. You may pray for someone's healing and nothing happens. But if you pray in love, you will have obeyed the highest commandment, even if there is no healing. Even when you feel absolutely *no* anointing, you can still be faithful to demonstrate the love of God, and God will honor that.

Real Life Testimony

Jane had been molested as a child. As a result, there were areas in her emotional life that had not developed as they should have.

Recently, when a ministry team member prayed for her, the Spirit of God came upon Jane with power, and she fell to the ground. While she lay there, God gave her a vision. In the vision, she was a little girl again. God took her and held her on His lap and told her He was imparting to her all of the things she had missed emotionally while growing up.

Since that time, there have been noticeable changes in Jane. There is a joy and emotional stability in her life that had not been there previously. She even looks different. Those who knew her before have commented that she seems to be getting younger! The Spirit of God has, in the words of

Isaiah, "bestow[ed] on [her] a crown of beauty instead of ashes, the oil of gladness instead of mourning, and a garment of praise instead of a spirit of despair" (Isa. 61:3,4).

In the short space of fifteen minutes, the power of God had accomplished what years of counseling could not. He healed her wounded emotions.

If you are empowered by the Spirit, God has called you to minister for Him. If you are not actively involved in ministry, why not pray right now and ask God to begin to give you opportunities to minister. He will!

When God leads you to people in need, don't feel you need to pretend to "know it all." Come with love and humility. If the person is sick, you can say something like this: "I'm so sorry you're sick. I'm a Christian, and I am learning that God answers prayer. Would you mind if I prayed for you right now?"

Very few people will refuse a request like that! If you don't see immediate results, don't worry. The results are God's job, not yours. Often the results of healing may take hours to manifest. If nothing happens immediately, just assure the person you will continue to pray for her. You will have shown that person the love of God and manifested His kingdom on the earth.

THE GIFTS OF THE SPIRIT: POWER TOOLS FOR EFFECTIVE SERVICE

John wanted a bookshelf unit in his living room. He had seen pictures in home magazines of floor-to-ceiling shelf units that not only held books, but were also beautiful pieces of furniture. John wanted a shelf unit like the ones in those pictures, but he couldn't afford to buy one of those expensive units. So he decided to build his own.

The problem was John didn't have any tools. His father offered to give him a very nice table saw, but power tools had always made him nervous. He'd heard stories about people accidentally cutting off their fingers with a table saw. He didn't like the noise and the sawdust, either. Power tools seemed dangerous and messy, and he didn't want anything to do with such equipment.

So John decided to build a shelf unit without tools. He first bought some boards. They weren't really the length he needed, but he felt he could make do with shorter shelves than he had wanted.

Then he bought some bricks. He made two stacks of bricks, about a foot high, and laid a board across the top. Then he made two more stacks of bricks on top of that and laid another board across. John kept adding layers until he had a shelf unit about four feet high. By then, the unit was so wobbly he was afraid to make it any higher for fear it would fall over.

John put his books on the shelves and stood back to admire his work. It wasn't a very beautiful piece of furniture. The ungainly stack of bricks and boards was a lot smaller than he had wanted it to be, and it didn't hold all his books. It wasn't very stable either, but still he was pretty proud of himself. He had a shelf unit, and he didn't have to use any tools to build it.

That's the story of much of the Church today. We look at the Church in the New Testament, and we want to have one just like it. But the tools the Father has provided for building His Church seem messy and frightening, so we try to build a church without them.

The "power tools" God has offered us are called spiritual gifts. They are abilities given by the Spirit, designed to equip us to build up the Church. The New Testament describes these gifts as vitally important for the effective construction of the Church. Paul's comment concerning the operation of the gifts is, "*All* of these things *must* be done" for the Church to be edified and built up (1 Cor. 14:26, italics mine).

But spiritual gifts can be messy, particularly when people are just learning to use them. On occasion they can also be dangerous. Power is always dangerous; if not used properly, people can get hurt.

But without spiritual gifts, the church we build can never achieve the stature and effectiveness of the New Testament Church.

VARIETIES OF GIFTS

A great deal of confusion persists in the Church today surrounding the subject of spiritual gifts. First, we must recognize there are many kinds of gifts we receive from God. Salvation is a gift from God (see Eph. 2:8). Jesus Himself is a gift from the Father (see John 3:16). The presence and power of the Holy Spirit among us is also a gift (see Acts 2:38). In a general sense, everything we have—or ever will have—is a gift from God (see Rom. 11:36).

More specifically, there are three kinds of gifts we call spiritual gifts. Paul described these three categories of gifts to the church at Corinth when he wrote:

> There are different kinds of *gifts*, but the same Spirit. There are different kinds of *service*, but the same Lord. There are different kinds of *working*, but the same God works all of them in all men (1 Cor. 12:4-6, italics mine).

These verses describe three kinds of spiritual gifts. Each of these is associated with a different member of the Trinity, yet each is a manifestation of the life of Jesus through His people.

"Different kinds of working." These are different approaches to meeting human needs. The Father places within each of us a motivation to minister in a particular way. For one it may be a desire to meet needs by giving instruction. To another it's a desire to minister by showing mercy to the hurting. To someone else it's a motivation to meet practical needs through sacrificial giving. To another it's a desire to give a corrective word to get someone's life on the right track. These desires to serve in various ways are gifts of God. I call them the *motivational* gifts. They are expressions of the heart of Jesus and are listed in Romans 12:6-8.

"Different kinds of gifts." The Greek word for "gifts" used here, *charisma*, refers to a miraculous faculty given by God.[1] The *charisma* are supernatural manifestations produced by the Holy Spirit. These include such gifts as healing, miracles, tongues and prophecy. I call these the ministry gifts. Through the operation of these *charisma*, Jesus continues His ministry of healing the sick, casting out demons and revealing the

compassion of the Father to humankind. These ministry gifts are described in 1 Corinthians 12—14.

"Different kinds of service." The Greek word translated here as "service" is *diakonia* and refers to an office or a position of service within the Body. These leadership roles are established by Jesus to equip His Church for healthy functioning. Expressions of the authority of Jesus, these offices are listed in Ephesians 4:7-13.

Some pastors and teachers read the three lists of spiritual gifts I have just mentioned—Romans 12, 1 Corinthians 12—14 and Ephesians 4—and lump them all together in one list of gifts of the Spirit. Closer study reveals, however, that these different kinds of gifts operate in very different ways. Let's take a closer look at each.

THE MOTIVATIONAL GIFTS

The motivational gifts described in Romans 12 are given by the Father and administered by the indwelling Spirit. As discussed in chapter 2, these include:

1. *Prophecy.* The motivation to correct error by revealing the mind and heart of God in a given situation.
2. *Serving.* The desire to invest time and effort in meeting the practical needs of others.
3. *Teaching.* The desire to communicate God's truth in order to give others understanding and direction.
4. *Encouraging.* The desire to encourage and motivate others in their walk with God.
5. *Giving.* The desire to sacrificially give to meet the needs of others.
6. *Leading.* The desire to coordinate the efforts of others to accomplish a God-given vision.
7. *Mercy.* The desire to express the compassion of Jesus toward the hurting and wounded.

Each believer will have one of these basic motivations as the primary driving force behind his or her ministry. In whatever situation you find yourself, your primary orientation will be either as a teacher, as a prophet, as a giver, as a leader, etc.

How do these gifts operate?

I once heard Bill Gothard give a helpful illustration: Suppose you are sitting down for a meal at a large table. Around the table are a number of Christians, each with a different motivational gift. Suddenly a little child spills a glass of milk. Each of the people at the table decides to take action to help in the situation. The action they take will be determined by the motivational gift God has given them.

The *prophet* may give correction, telling the child he was wrong not to be paying attention to what he was doing.

The *teacher* will give instruction. He will point out to the child that if he sets the glass farther back from the edge of the table, it will not be as likely to spill the next time.

The *giver* will run to get the child another glass of milk. When the giver sees a need, his basic motivation is to meet it.

The person with the gift of *serving* will mop up the milk.

The person who shows *mercy* will be hugging the child and consoling him, so he doesn't feel so bad about the spilled milk.

That's how the motivational gifts function. The motivational gifts are all aspects of the character of Jesus. They each express one important facet of the character of Jesus in the life of a believer. Every Christian receives at least one of these gifts at the moment of salvation.

THE MINISTRY GIFTS

The ministry gifts, or *charisma*, are manifestations of the power of God released to His people to equip them for service. The Word describes them in this way:

To one there is given through the Spirit the word of wisdom, to another the word of knowledge by means of the same Spirit, to another faith by the same Spirit, to another gifts of healing by that one Spirit, to another miraculous powers, to another prophecy, to another distinguishing between spirits, to another speaking in different kinds of tongues, and to still another the interpretation of tongues (1 Cor. 12:8-10).

When you are empowered by the Holy Spirit, that power will find expression through you in the various *charisma* of the Spirit.

The Word of Wisdom. "Wisdom" means "skill in living." It's the ability to solve problems and deal skillfully with situations to bring about the desired outcome. The word of wisdom is revelation from God that provides *supernatural* wisdom. Kevin Conner calls it "a flash of revelation given by the Spirit."[2] Owen Weston describes it as an "instant insight" that shows "how a given situation or need is to be resolved or helped or healed."[3]

A good biblical example of this gift is found in Mark 12:14-17. The Pharisees thought they had devised the perfect trap for Jesus. They asked Him if it was right for God's people to pay taxes to Caesar. If He said yes, He would alienate the Jewish people, who hated the Romans. If He said no, the Romans would arrest Him for teaching the people not to pay their taxes.

In this seemingly no-win situation, however, Jesus found a unique answer. Operating in supernatural wisdom from the Holy Spirit, Jesus demanded that the Pharisees tell Him whose image was on a Roman coin. "Caesar's," they replied. He instructed them, "Give to Caesar what belongs to Caesar and give to God what belongs to God."

The Pharisees fully understood what Jesus was saying. Even as that coin bore Caesar's image, every human being carries God's image. We can give to Caesar the taxes he demands, but God demands our hearts! The wisdom of Jesus' answer was so profound it left His adversaries without a response. Mark tells us "they were *amazed* at Him" (v. 17, italics mine).

The Word of Knowledge. The word of knowledge is not the ability to study, research or gain knowledge through natural means; it is a word from God that brings knowledge. Owen Weston calls it "a revelation of facts about a person or situation which is not learned through the efforts of the natural mind, but is a fragment of knowledge freely given by God."[4]

For example, in conversing with the Samaritan woman at the well, Jesus received from the Holy Spirit a piece of information He had no natural way of knowing: She had had five husbands and was not married to the man she was presently living with. That piece of information broke through her pretense and opened the door for revival in an entire village (see John 4:16-39).

Faith. C. Peter Wagner describes the gift of faith as the ability "to discern with extraordinary confidence the will and purposes of God for the future of His work."[5] When you operate in the gift of faith, you *know* what God desires, and you are supremely confident that no matter how negative the circumstances, God will make it possible.

In 1992, the Lord told me and my wife to take our three children on a mission trip to Ukraine. After much prayer, we felt we had clearly heard from the Lord, so we began making preparations for the trip, applying for the children's passports and so forth. And yet we were met by delays at every turn.

The first problem was financial. The total cost of the trip would be more than $10,000. We sent letters to the people who usually support our ministry, and money slowly began to come in, but nothing near what we needed. One week before our departure, we were still $5,000 short. We knew that if we went forward with the trip, we could end up $5,000 in debt.

The other major problem was with our visas. We could not apply for the visas until all the children had passports, and the passport for one of our children was several weeks late in arriving.

When that passport finally came, we sent off the application for the visas, but again we were met with a long delay.

One week before we were due to leave, we still had no visas. For travel into the newly formed Commonwealth of Independent States at that time, you could not board the plane without proper visas in hand. If the day of the flight came and we had no visas, we would simply forfeit the $10,000 we had spent on plane tickets.

The deadline to cancel the trip and get a refund on the tickets came five days before our departure date. As that day approached, our friends cautioned us that we could end up deeply in debt and still be unable to make the trip if the visas did not arrive.

We went before the Lord in prayer, and the Lord spoke clearly to us. "You WILL go!" With that word, God released to us the gift of faith. No matter how impossible the situation looked, we *knew* God had said to go and that *somehow* He would make it possible.

We committed to go, and within two days the remaining $5,000 came in! That was a real encouragement, but we still had no visas. Every day we called the visa office in Dallas, but every day we received the same reply: The visas had not yet arrived, but could come any day. The night before we were scheduled to leave, we packed all the suitcases and set them in the hallway just inside our front door. We still had no visas.

We were scheduled to leave for the airport at 9:00 the next morning. At 8:30 A.M., the phone rang. It was the visa office. They were sending a courier to the airport to meet us at the gate with our visas!

That trip proved to be a tremendous time of ministry. It had a life-changing impact on our children, but more than that, it was a tremendous testimony to God's faithfulness to His promise. Looking back, I am amazed we had the faith to walk through that situation. But the faith we exercised was not our own. It was God's supernatural provision—a *gift* of faith.

Healings. Leslie Flynn defines the gift of healing as "the ability to intervene in a supernatural way as an instrument for the curing of illness and restoration of health."[6] It should be noted that in the Greek text, the words for "gift" and "healing" are both plural. There are a variety of healing gifts given by God, and we will study more about these gifts in chapter 11.

Miracles. The word translated "miraculous powers" in 1 Corinthians 12:10 is the Greek word *dunamis*. It is a reference to the supernatural power of God. Frank Damazio defines this gift as the ability to perform "what is naturally impossible through the power of God."[7] R. M. Riggs describes a miracle as "an orderly intervention in the regular operations of nature."[8] Technically speaking, a miracle is not the suspension of natural law, but the overcoming of the forces of nature through the application of divine power.

The ministry of Jesus provides many illustrations of this gift, including walking on water, multiplying resources to feed multitudes and raising the dead.

Prophecy. C. Peter Wagner defines prophecy as the ability "to receive and communicate an immediate message of God to His people through a divinely anointed utterance."[9] We will take a closer look at the gift of prophecy in chapter 10.

Distinguishing Spirits. The gift of distinguishing or discerning spirits is not the same as general discernment. Discerning spirits involves the supernatural ability to discern the forces in the spiritual realm that are influencing activities in the natural realm. Frank Damazio defines this gift as the ability to recognize "what spirit (divine, evil or human) is causing a certain manifestation or activity."[10]

When Jesus turned to Peter in Matthew 16:23 and said, "Get behind me, Satan!" He was looking beyond the natural realm into the spiritual. He recognized that Peter was, at that moment, being influenced in his thoughts and words by Satan. Discerning the demonic spirit behind Peter's statement, Jesus addressed Satan directly and rebuked him.

Tongues. The gift of tongues is the ability to "speak by the

Spirit in a language that he has not previously learned."[11] We will look more closely at this gift in chapter 9.

Interpretation of Tongues. The gift of interpretation of tongues is "the divine enablement to make known to the body the message of one who is speaking in tongues."[12] The interpretation of a tongue is not necessarily a word-for-word translation, but rather a prophetic interpretation of what the tongue is communicating. One who interprets tongues may hear the actual words in English as the tongue is being spoken. At other times, they simply get the "sense" of what is being said.

LEVELS OF OPERATION

These nine ministry gifts operate on two levels. The first level on which these gifts operate is that of a *momentary unction*, or anointing. At a given point in time, the Spirit of God may release an anointing through one of His people to operate in any of these gifts.

We should all come to church prepared to function in any of the gifts!

We see this level of operation described in 1 Corinthians 12:7-11. In this passage, Paul describes a group of Christians coming together in the church. He says that as God's people come together (assuming there is freedom for the gifts to operate) God may give to one person gifts of healing, to another He may give an anointing to prophesy, to another He may give a tongue, etc. God sovereignly manifests His gifts; His people can never know which gifts will be manifested through which person.

On this level, all these gifts are available to all Christians. On any occasion, the Spirit can manifest any gift through any Christian who is open to it. Paul makes it clear that in this context *all* can speak in tongues, *all* can interpret, *all* can prophesy (see 1 Cor. 14:5,13,18,26,31). We should all come to church prepared to function in any of the gifts!

Paul's primary ministry was as an apostle, yet he frequently healed the sick, cast out demons, prophesied, spoke in tongues, taught and received words of knowledge. (See, for example, 1 Cor. 14:6,18.) On several occasions, Paul strongly exhorts all Christians to seek to operate in all the gifts and to pray for additional gifts (see 1 Cor. 12:31; 14:1,13,39).

The second level on which the *charisma* operate is that of an *ongoing ministry* (see 1 Cor. 12:27-31). While any Spirit-filled Christian *may* operate in any of these gifts on occasion, God will give each obedient Christian an ongoing ministry in at least one of these areas.

When God calls a believer to function in one of these gifts on a regular basis, that becomes known as "their gift," or "their ministry." Some have an ongoing ministry of healing, others of teaching, others of prophesying and so on. On this level, 1 Corinthians 12:27-31 indicates no one ministry will be given to all Christians (e.g., not all will be prophets or teachers or healers).

THE LEADERSHIP GIFTS

The leadership gifts, or offices, are given by Jesus to the Church to equip God's people to do the work of ministry. A church will be hindered in its ministry if all of these offices are not in place.

The Apostle. The apostle has an anointing to set the church in order so all of the gifts may function effectively. The apostle often has a ministry of church planting. He may also have a ministry of apostolic oversight to more than one church.

The Prophet. The prophet receives accurate revelation from God and has the maturity to handle this revelation wisely. He will help give guidance and direction to the church, as well as helping to establish the revelatory gifts—prophecy, tongues, interpretation, word of knowledge, word of wisdom—in the Body.

The Evangelist. The evangelist not only wins many to the Lord, but also encourages and trains others to effectively draw men and women to Jesus. The evangelist also establishes the power gifts—such as healing, faith and miracles—in the Body.

The Pastor. The pastor is a shepherd; he gives personal care to the members of the flock. He will have a broad overview of the condition of the sheep and a vision from God of where the church should be going.

The Teacher. The teacher gives the church and its members stability and helps them grow to maturity by supplying the strong foundation of the truth of God.

Every believer benefits from the presence of these offices, but only a handful of Christians are called to occupy them.

GROWTH IN THE GIFTS

When it comes to the gifts of the Holy Spirit, many Christians think, *Some people have them. Some people don't. It's God's choice, and there's nothing we can do.* They assume that if you don't have a powerful gifting now, you may as well sit back and leave the job of ministry to those who do. But that's not what the Bible says about spiritual gifts.

The Bible describes the functioning of the gifts as a process of growth. We are encouraged to stir up and exercise the gifts we have (see 2 Tim. 1:6), to pray for and seek additional gifts and to impart spiritual gifts from one believer to another. We should be developing proficiency in using more and more of the Spirit's gifts so we can be more and more effective in serving Jesus.

How do we learn to operate in these gifts? Consider the example of "Joe Christian." Joe is a brand-new baby Christian coming to your church for the first time. He's full of enthusiasm, he loves the Lord, and he wants to serve God. He has the Holy Spirit living within him, and you pray for him to be empowered by the Spirit. But Joe doesn't know how to do *anything* yet. How does he learn to operate in the spiritual gifts?

The Bible suggests the following progression in the operation of the Gifts:

Stage One:

THE MOTIVATIONAL GIFTS IN OPERATION

The Bible says that some Christians are "unlearned" in spiritual charisma (see 1 Cor. 14:23). That's where Joe is; he doesn't understand anything about the Spirit's operation. An unlearned Christian may be filled with the Spirit, but does not yet understand how to function in the gifts.

Because of their ignorance of gifts, these Christians may be confused or even offended when they see gifts in operation. Unfortunately, in the Church today, there are many longtime Christians who still fall into this category.

While unlearned Christians don't yet know how to function in the *charisma*, they do have a motivational gift from God. That motivational gift, if they yield to the Spirit, will give them a desire to reach out and minister.

Let's suppose Joe Christian's motivational gift is mercy. As he sees people in need, he reaches out to them. He will go to a brother in need and pray with him. He will express the love of Jesus.

That is the first level of operation in the gifts. It is not supernatural; it is simply obedient service motivated by the indwelling Holy Spirit.

Stage Two:

THE MINISTRY GIFTS AS MOMENTARY UNCTIONS

As Joe continues to obediently serve God through his motivational gift, he begins to notice that, on occasion, when he prays for someone, God acts through him in a supernatural way. He may be praying for a sister who is sick, and God works in power to heal her. He may be praying for a brother in distress, and God gives Joe a prophetic word to encourage him. Joe has now begun to operate in the *charisma*, or ministry gifts, but only as momentary unctions.

This should be a normal experience in the life of a new Christian. When a person is filled with the Holy Spirit, the giftings of the Spirit will begin to manifest through him. He (or she) will have visions or words of knowledge. New Christians may find themselves praying with words they do not understand. They may have strange sensations of heat or energy in their hands when they pray for the sick. They will probably experience many of these manifestations from time to time.

If they have been taught, they will learn to recognize what the Spirit is doing in these situations and begin to function in these gifts to great benefit. If they have not been taught about the gifts of the Spirit, they may experience these for years but not know what to do about it.

Stage Three:

A MINISTRY GIFT AS AN ONGOING MINISTRY

As Joe continues to mature in the Lord and obediently serves Him, he finds there is one gift that God begins to manifest regularly through him.

Let's suppose that for Joe, as he ministers from his motivational gift of mercy, God begins to regularly give him accurate prophetic words. The leadership of his church begins to take notice that his prophetic words are effective in ministering to people, and the church encourages him in this gift. Eventually, as he continues to grow and mature, he is acknowledged as having a ministry in prophecy. (Note: This does not mean he is a prophet. He doesn't yet have the maturity or authority of a prophet. He does, however, have an effective ministry in prophecy.)

Again, this should be a normal part of a Christian's growth. As a believer walks in obedient service, he will find there are one or two gifts God manifests through him on a fairly regular basis. This gift will be different for different believers. Some will find that the sick are healed almost every time they pray for them. Some will find they frequently receive visions and words of knowledge. Some will find that God supernaturally opens up His Word to them to reveal His truth.

When God allows you to exercise a ministry gift on a regular, ongoing basis, He is calling you to a ministry in that area. Ministry does not necessarily mean a full-time job; it means an effective avenue of service.

You will still have many occasions to grow in other gifts, but your primary function in the church will be in the area of your ministry. It is important that you not be impatient as this develops. Submit to the leadership of your church and allow them to "exalt" you in this ministry at the proper time.

Stage Four:

THE GIFT AS AN OFFICE

Many years have passed, and Joe has continued to grow in the Lord, walking a humble and obedient walk. As he continues to minister in prophecy, there comes a time when God brings him into a new level of authority. His prophetic words carry a new weight, and he has a new level of discernment. God has moved him into the *office* of prophet.

Again, this should be a normal occurrence in the church. When a Christian's functioning in a ministry gift is constant and beneficial over many years, the time may come when God exalts him or her to a higher level of authority. The church will say, "We recognize publicly that this person has the office of prophet (or teacher, or apostle, etc.)." A person with this level of maturity and proficiency in the gifts is one who can not only operate in the gift himself, but can also train others to exercise it, and is of great benefit to the Church at large.

PROVIDING A GROWTH ENVIRONMENT

The growth process is important to recognize and to nurture in your church. Rarely will someone who is baptized in the Spirit immediately operate in a gift with great proficiency. Proficiency in the gifts takes time. It takes growth. One who is learning to exercise gifts will make mistakes.

To "grow a church" full of people who function with maturity in the gifts, the people must be cared for and nurtured like plants in a garden. They must have the opportunity to try to exercise the gifts without fear of rejection. If they are wrong, or are ministering in a way that is harmful, they must be gently corrected and encouraged to try again (see 2 Tim. 4:2).

Unfortunately, many churches do not provide a good environment for people to grow in the area of gifts. In many church activities, only one or two people are given any opportunity to speak or minister, usually only those who have already shown themselves to be proficient in ministry.

In Paul's first letter to the Corinthians, he describes a New Testament church meeting. Try to picture what it was like:

When you come together, *everyone* has a hymn, or a word of instruction, a revelation, a tongue or an interpretation. All of these must be done for the strengthening of the church. If anyone speaks in a tongue, two—or at the most three—should speak, one at a time, and someone must interpret. If there is no interpreter, the speaker should keep quiet in the church and speak to himself and God.

Two or three prophets should speak, and the others should weigh carefully what is said. And if a revelation comes to someone who is sitting down, the first speaker should stop. For you can all prophesy in turn so that everyone may be instructed and encouraged (1 Cor. 14:26-31, italics mine).

The meeting described here was not a formal worship service where hundreds of people gathered to praise God and hear the Bible taught. I believe this was a smaller group, perhaps only 20 or 30 people who came together before the Lord in a more informal setting.

Everyone at this meeting had the freedom to participate. In fact, they were not only *free* to participate, they were *exhorted* to be involved. Each one could prophesy, speak in tongues or give a teaching. They were all to come prepared to do it all!

History tells us the Early Church probably began their meetings with joyful singing and praise, then invited the Spirit of God to pour out His gifts. The people were free to respond to the Spirit. One might give a brief word in a tongue (see v. 27). If a tongue was given, the group would wait for the interpretation. If there was no one present who could give the interpretation, there could be no more tongues at that meeting. If an interpretation was given, others could speak in a tongue, although not more than three in any one meeting (see vv. 27,28).

Those who received revelation from God—a prophecy, a vision, a word of knowledge—would be free to share it. When something was said, it would be tested by the others there (see v. 29). If what was said "bore witness" with the others as a valid word from God, they would all confirm it by answering "Amen" (see 1 Cor. 14:16).

Ministry needed to be done in an orderly fashion. The worshipers were careful not to interrupt each other (see 1 Cor. 14:30-32). If a vision or word of knowledge came, they would pray for an interpretation.

From Paul's description of the use of spiritual gifts in 1 Corinthians 12, it is clear that other ministry also took place at these meetings. If one was sick, others might gather around and lay their hands on him and pray for healing. If one was in need, the others would pray in faith for God to work.

This kind of meeting was evidently very common in the Early Church. It provided a setting where people could learn to recognize the voice of God and learn to operate in His anointings. I believe it is vital for the Church today to have times where this kind of growth environment is re-created.

GROWTH THROUGH SMALL GROUPS

It is very difficult to learn to operate in the spiritual gifts without personal guidance and instruction. The New Testament describes growth in the gifts as taking place in a *corporate* setting. One of the exciting things God is doing in our day is calling the Church back to the importance of small group meetings. This is an ideal place to learn to operate in the gifts.

If you have access to this kind of a group in your church, join it! If your church does not have this kind of meeting, speak with your pastor about the possibility of starting one. *Be sure to get permission from your pastor before you try to begin such a group!* God will not honor your efforts if you fail to respect the leadership He has given His church.

If your pastor is agreeable to the formation of a small group for the purpose of growing in the spiritual gifts, here are some suggestions for establishing such a meeting:

1. Begin by teaching about the gifts and the way gifts operate in the church.

2. Set a time and meet together for the purpose of learning to exercise the gifts.

3. The leader of the group should be the pastor of the church or someone else approved by the pastor.

4. The leader should establish an open, accepting atmosphere for the meeting. People need to know it's okay to make mistakes. They need to know that if they think they hear God, it is okay to share what they hear. At the same time, the leader must have the authority and firmness to keep things on track. If someone is disorderly or doing something that may be harmful to others, he or she must be corrected.

5. Each person is to come prepared. This means spending time with the Lord at some point before the meeting to listen to what God is saying. Members of the group should come prepared to share, not just receive.

6. Begin the meeting with a time of praise and worship. During this time, be sensitive and seek the Spirit's presence. Maintain an atmosphere of worship. When the leader senses the presence of the Holy Spirit, he or she should pray and invite the Spirit of God to manifest Himself through His gifts.

7. Give people the freedom to share, and let them receive feedback from the others so they can know if they are ministering effectively. Don't be afraid of periods of silence. Learn to wait on the Lord and gain sensitivity to His presence. Try to sense the "flow" of the Spirit, and discern the overall message the Holy Spirit desires to communicate at that meeting.

8. Point out to the people what the Spirit is doing. Help them recognize when the Spirit has come upon someone in the group. Have them pray for those to whom the Spirit is ministering.
9. At some point, ask if there is anyone sick or in need. As the Spirit leads, have the group gather around and lay hands on any sick person and pray for healing.

The first time you meet, people may be a little uncomfortable. That's okay. Any time you try something new, some people will be uneasy. Meet together in a group like this every week for several months and you will be surprised how quickly you all grow in your ability to function in the gifts of the Spirit.

PRAYING IN THE SPIRIT: THE MOST CONTROVERSIAL GIFT

I met Kostya on my first visit to Moscow in 1991. Kostya pastors a large Russian Pentecostal church in that city and has been a great help to me on several occasions when I was there. Although from our first meeting I felt an immediate bond of friendship with Kostya, we have always had a difficult time communicating. Kostya knows no English, and my Russian is very limited. Fortunately, Kostya's wife, Helena, speaks English very well, although with a pronounced British accent. (She spent a year studying at a Bible school in England.)

In 1993, while on a missions trip to Russia, my schedule permitted me to be in Moscow on a Sunday for the first time, and Kostya invited me to speak in his church. His church met at that time in an old Communist party meeting hall. It was a huge auditorium with the hammer and sickle still in place over the stage, but the people who crowded in were hungry for Jesus!

As Kostya began the service, he stepped to the microphone, raised his hands and began to pray—in clear, unaccented American English. "Holy Spirit of God, we welcome you here today..."

As his prayer continued, my mouth dropped open. If you've spent any time with Russians, you know it's nearly impossible for a Russian to speak in unaccented English without many years of training and practice. Yet Kostya had never studied English!

After the service I talked with Helena and said, "I thought Kostya didn't know English. He was praying in perfect English during the church service!"

She smiled, "Oh! He doesn't know English. That's his prayer language. He didn't understand anything he said!"

She went on to explain that when she and Kostya were dating, she would always know what was on his heart since, when they prayed together, he would pray "in tongues" in English and she, knowing English, could understand everything he was praying!

That was my first encounter with someone who did not know English speaking fluent English "in tongues." I have since experienced this on several other occasions and it always fills me with amazement! When I heard Kostya speak, I caught a glimpse of what the crowd must have felt in Acts chapter 2 when they heard foreigners speaking messages from God in their native languages. It has given me a fresh appreciation of that most controversial gift, the gift of tongues. In this chapter, I want to discuss the purpose of this peculiar gift, and try to answer some of the questions I am frequently asked about it.

As I mentioned before, I spent much of my life in churches where any kind of "speaking in tongues" was forbidden. I was taught against the validity of tongues in seminary. As a result, when I began to minister, I also taught against tongues. For the first ten years of my ministry, I would preach sermons against tongues several times a year.

Then, without either of us seeking it, God gave my wife and me the gift of tongues. Literally overnight, the presence of the Lord invaded our home. In the midst of that wonderful time, God met with each of us in a special way and released in us the gift of tongues.

At first, it was very hard for me to talk about this experience. I had been taught against tongues for so long, it was hard to admit I was now one of "those people." When I finally began to tell people of my experience with this gift, there were many who rejected me and cut off fellowship because of it. In spite of this, however, I have never regretted speaking in tongues. I can testify that in all of my years of walking with God, I have found nothing that has given me closer fellowship with the Lord than praying in tongues.

In the years since, I have gained more and more appreciation for this wonderful work of the Spirit. I pray in tongues all the time. I don't think there has been a day in the last fourteen years that I have not spoken in tongues. I pray in tongues when I go to bed at night. I pray in tongues when I get up in the morning. I pray in tongues during my personal quiet time. I pray in tongues when I drive down the street in my car. I cannot imagine trying to walk with the Lord without this gift. I have found that it is *always* a means of entering into a deep intimacy with Jesus.

THE BIBLICAL ATTITUDE TOWARD TONGUES

While many Christians today speak negatively about tongues, the Bible has always spoken very positively about this gift.

In Acts 2, *every one* of the apostles spoke in tongues.

In 1 Corinthians, Paul thanks God that he speaks in tongues, and expresses his desire for *every Christian* to speak in tongues.

We're told that speaking in tongues will edify or strengthen our spirits (see 1 Cor. 14:4; Jude 20).

In Ephesians 6:18 we are exhorted to pray in the Spirit *on all occasions.*

The New Testament was written by people who spoke in tongues. In the New Testament Church, speaking in tongues was considered a normal activity for all Christians. Because the New Testament so stresses the importance of tongues, we should examine carefully the biblical teaching about this gift.

BASIC QUESTIONS ABOUT TONGUES

For those who don't speak in tongues, the gift of tongues is often a mysterious and frightening thing. Some people fear that if they speak in tongues, they might lose control and speak in tongues at inappropriate times. Others have asked me whether a person loses consciousness when speaking in tongues!

Because of the many misconceptions out there, let's begin by answering some of the frequently asked questions about tongues.

WHAT IS "SPEAKING IN TONGUES"?

The gift of tongues is simply the God-given capacity for your spirit to express itself in words your mind does not understand.

The Bible indicates that "tongues" are not meaningless, uncontrolled babbling. The Greek word used to describe speaking in tongues is the word for "language." Speaking in tongues involves your spirit expressing specific thoughts in a language you don't know.

ARE TONGUES REAL LANGUAGES?

Some have assumed the term "unknown language" means that tongues are not real languages. That is not accurate. An "unknown" tongue is simply a language unknown to the speaker.

The question of whether a tongue will be understood by the hearers is largely dependent on who the hearers are. In Acts 2, tongues were understood by the hearers because the hearers were from many different countries. In the local church at

Corinth, the tongues were unknown because the hearers were all from the same country and did not have the linguistic diversity found in the crowd that gathered on the day of Pentecost.

If I stood up in the General Assembly of the United Nations and gave a message in Swahili, chances are very good it would be recognized and understood by a number of people present. If I gave the same message in an average, small-town church in Texas, however, it would probably be an unknown language to everyone present.

Many times today tongues *are* recognized by the hearers, just as they were in Acts 2. As I mentioned, I have found myself in several situations where I have heard people praying "in tongues" in English—people who otherwise knew no English. It is always an impressive experience. It's no wonder the people on the day of Pentecost were so shaken to hear uneducated Galileans speaking in their native languages!

Many Christians who pray in tongues don't really appreciate what a miraculous gift it is. It seems so natural to speak in a tongue, it's easily taken for granted. I have a Russian friend, Anna, who was saved as a result of an experience with the gift of tongues. Anna grew up in the Tartar Republic of the U.S.S.R. in a Moslem family. She was trained as a linguist in college and later became a language teacher. In the late 1980s, she was invited by a friend to a Pentecostal church.

During the service, Anna was perplexed that people were speaking in such a variety of languages. Because of her linguistic training, she recognized one person praying in Latin, another in German.

Following the service, she asked her friend why people were praying in different languages. When her friend explained the gift of tongues, and that the people speaking did not understand what they were saying, Anna was so impressed by this supernatural gift that she gave her heart to Jesus!

Why don't we recognize the tongue being spoken more

often? We need to remember that there are thousands of languages in the world today. In addition, there have been many more thousands of languages down through history that have either died out or changed so drastically as to be unrecognizable today. Even a trained linguist would only recognize a small fraction of the total number of human languages, yet when God gives a tongue, it could potentially be in any of these languages. First Corinthians 13:1 suggests the possibility that some tongues may actually be *angelic* languages. In the light of the great diversity of human languages, it is actually surprising that specific tongues are recognized by a hearer as often as they are!

DOES A PERSON "LOSE CONTROL" WHEN HE SPEAKS IN TONGUES?

To speak in tongues is a conscious, rational choice. One who speaks in tongues can choose to speak in tongues at any time, or choose to remain silent. While there are times when you may feel "prompted" by the Spirit to exercise tongues, you always have the ability to choose. "The spirits of prophets are subject to the control of prophets" (1 Cor. 14:32).

I like to compare the choice to pray in tongues with the choice to express yourself in song. The ability to sing is always there. If you are able to sing at all, you can choose to sing at any time. There are times, however, when it feels very natural to sing, when a song rises within you almost spontaneously. That's how it is with tongues.

WHY PRAY IN TONGUES?

What is the point in praying when you don't understand your own words? Some assume the purpose of tongues is for evangelism, to enable a speaker to communicate the gospel to those who don't share a common language. There is no hint in the New Testament that this gift was ever used for that purpose.

In the New Testament world, Greek was a universal language. Nearly anyone in the Roman empire could have understood a message spoken in Greek. On the day of Pentecost, for example, even though the people heard the apostles praising God in a variety of languages, Peter could proclaim the gospel in Greek with full confidence that all those present would understand.

In that setting, while tongues were not necessary for communication, they did serve as a supernatural sign. Those who heard the outpouring of tongues understood they were witnessing a miraculous manifestation. The supernatural nature of this gift helped draw them to Jesus, just as it did for my friend Anna.

But the primary purpose for tongues is to be a private prayer language for intense communication between your spirit and the Lord. Paul boasts that while he spoke in tongues more than any of the Corinthians, his primary use of tongues was in prayer to God (see 1 Cor. 14:15,19). He calls this expression of prayer praying "in the Spirit" (Eph. 6:18). Some have questioned whether praying in the Spirit is the same as praying in tongues. Paul answers this question in the affirmative when he says in 1 Corinthians 14:16 that if you pray in the Spirit, those who are listening will not be able to understand what you are saying.

In this same passage, Paul contrasts praying in the spirit with praying with understanding. I think it's important for us to understand this distinction.

When you pray with understanding, your voice is an expression of the thoughts in your mind. Your mind provides the *content* of what you pray. You are choosing to open your mouth and operate your vocal chords to express the thoughts of your mind in audible words.

Prayer with understanding is good, valid and important (see 1 Cor. 14:15). It is not "unspiritual" to pray with understanding. Yet even as you pray with the mind, the Spirit can direct your prayer. He may give you visions, prophetic words or words of knowledge to help you pray more specifically.

When you pray in tongues, your voice is an expression of your spirit. Your spirit communicates directly with the Father, free of the limitations and distractions of your mind.

When you pray with the spirit, on the other hand, the content of the prayer is provided not by your mind, but by your spirit. You are still choosing to speak. Your mind is still conscious and aware, but the mind is "unfruitful" (1 Cor. 14:14). It is not supplying, nor even understanding the words that are spoken.

When you pray in tongues, your voice is an expression of your spirit. Your spirit is free to communicate directly with the Father without going through the filter of your mind.

The Bible gives us several reasons why it is important to pray in tongues:

Prayer in tongues will edify your spirit. A time of intimacy with God through praying in your spirit will recharge your spiritual batteries. It will strengthen your spirit and draw you closer to God.

Prayer in tongues will enable your praying. There are many times when you feel you need to pray, but your mind is too tired or preoccupied to concentrate. There are other times you sense a need to pray, but you don't know exactly *what* to pray. You know your spirit wants to pray, but your mind lacks the specific knowledge to pray effectively. At times such as these, praying in tongues is extremely helpful. "Spirit-assisted prayer" allows your spirit to express itself directly to God, without being limited by the mind's knowledge or ability.

The gift of tongues will enable your praising. The ability to speak in tongues makes it possible for you to express your praise to God when your mind is inadequate to do it. At times your spirit is filled with such overwhelming love for God, and you want to express praise to Him, but you are frustrated by your inability to find the right words. That's what Wesley felt when he wrote his hymn, "O for a Thousand Tongues!" Wesley was saying that he felt unable to express his praise adequately. He wished for more ways to express it. This is one of the purposes of tongues, to allow your spirit to express itself in praise when your mind is inadequate to do so. Paul writes about singing in tongues and praising in tongues, as well as praying in tongues (see 1 Cor. 14:15,16).

The gift of tongues equips you to stand against your spiritual enemy. In his letter to the Ephesians, after listing the spiritual armor God has provided us, Paul exhorts Christians to pray in the Spirit constantly when times of spiritual warfare come (see Eph. 6:18).

WHO CAN SPEAK IN TONGUES?

I believe any Christian who is filled with the Holy Spirit has the potential to speak in tongues.

The New Testament presents speaking in tongues as a *normal* activity for those who are filled with the Spirit. A number of passages indicate that the first outward sign of the Spirit's empowering was the release of tongues (see Acts 2:4; 10:44-46; 19:6). The apostle Paul also implied that speaking in tongues is available to *all* Christians (see 1 Cor. 14:23,26).

Some have misinterpreted Paul's question in 1 Corinthians 12:30—"Do all speak in tongues?"—to mean that the gift of tongues is not available to all. Literally translated, his question is "All are not speakers in tongues, are they?" But this objection fails to consider the context of his question. In this passage, Paul is dealing with the gifts not simply as manifestations of the Holy Spirit, but as ministries God has appointed in the Church.

Paul is simply saying that each of us has been called to a different area of ministry (see Rom. 12:4). Not all have been called to be teachers. Not all have been called to be prophets. Not all have been called to minister to the church in public messages of tongues. He does not imply, however, that all Christians cannot function in any of those gifts on occasion.

The fact that not everyone is called to be a teacher does not mean that God will not use all Christians to teach (see Heb. 5:12). The fact that not everyone is called to be a healer does not mean that God cannot use every Christian to pray for the sick and see them healed. The fact that not everyone is a prophet (see 1 Cor. 12:29) does not negate the fact that all can prophesy (see 1 Cor. 14:31).

The fact that not all are called to a ministry in tongues (see 1 Cor. 12:30) does not negate the fact that all can pray in tongues (see 1 Cor. 14:5,18,23).

Both the Bible and the common experience of many Christians testify that all the gifts, including tongues, are intended for use by every believer. I believe that any Spirit-filled Christian who wants to speak in tongues can do it.

It is a normal, natural activity to pray in the Spirit. The only Christians who usually have any difficulty beginning to speak in tongues are those who have been taught against it. If you desire to do it, you can!

HOW CAN I BE RELEASED IN THE GIFT OF TONGUES?
I like to speak of people "being released" in the gift of tongues rather than "receiving" the gift of tongues. In a real sense, if you are a Spirit-filled Christian, you don't have to pray for tongues to receive it. You *have* it. It is part of the package you received when you received the filling of the Spirit. The Holy Spirit within you comes with all the gifts as standard equipment. You might picture the gift of tongues as being "locked up" inside you. It just needs to be released.

WHY DON'T ALL CHRISTIANS SPEAK IN TONGUES?

So why don't all Christians speak in tongues today? There are several reasons. Some Christians are not *filled* with the Spirit. Out of ignorance, false teaching or stubbornness, many Christians have never experienced the empowering of the Spirit. If you're not empowered by the Spirit, the gifts of the Spirit will not be at your disposal.

There are some Christians who dearly love the Lord and are clearly empowered by the Spirit, but have never been *released* in the gift of tongues. Some do not know what the Bible teaches about tongues; they don't even know they can speak in tongues.

Other Christians are bound up in *intellectualism*. Many today have an overintellectualized Christianity. They have allowed a relationship with Jesus to be reduced to a system of doctrines. They have been taught that the guiding principle of the Christian life is human reason. Anything the mind cannot understand is suspect. They forget that God *chooses* the foolish things of the world to shame the wise (see 1 Cor. 1:27). He chooses to confound the mind in order to test the heart.

The intellectual's focus is so much on the mind, he or she has little awareness of the spiritual realm. Because of this, it is very difficult for their minds to yield control of the mouth to the Spirit. Such people often have a difficult time learning to pray in tongues.

Fear holds many back, preventing them from being released to pray in the Spirit. For many, it is the fear of *deception*. Some Christians have been told that tongues are of Satan. They say, "If I ask for tongues, how do I know I'm not going to get something from the devil? I can't even understand what I'm saying!"

To answer this fear, we need to remind such a person that if there were a danger in receiving tongues, God would certainly have warned us about it in the Bible. Yet God never speaks of seeking His gifts as a dangerous thing. In fact, in Luke 11:11-13, Jesus says just the opposite. He assures us if we ask God for His good gifts, He will not allow us to receive something evil or harmful.

For some, a fear of the unknown prevents them from being released to pray in the Spirit. For them, tongues is something unknown and mysterious. Many Christians have never heard someone speak in tongues. Some don't even know anyone who does.

Because the gift of tongues is an unknown for them, such Christians have all sorts of strange ideas about the practice. Some imagine if they speak in tongues, they will go into a trance; or they may lose control and speak in tongues at a business meeting!

That is a false picture of tongues. Speaking in tongues is not mystical; it is very natural. When speaking in tongues, you are conscious and in control. You can start at any time and stop at any time. You can interrupt the flow of tongues to speak in your own language. It does not have to be an overly emotional experience.

Speaking in tongues is just a matter of "shifting gears." It is the same kind of internal gear shifting that takes place when you stop talking and begin singing. Once you have been released in it, it is a very natural thing to do.

Speaking in tongues can seem so natural, Satan often comes to a person within the first few weeks he or she is speaking in tongues and makes false accusations. He says, "That's not the real thing. You're faking it!"

The evidence that the gift of tongues is valid and from God comes from the fruit it yields. Though a "natural" activity, it produces supernatural results. As you continue to pray in tongues over a period of time, you will find changes taking place in your life. You will find you have a deeper sense of fellowship with God, a greater sensitivity to the Spirit and a greater desire to praise and serve Him.

Finally, there is the basic human fear of looking foolish or being rejected. Many Christians *have* been rejected by their former Christian friends when they set their hearts on seeking God and His gifts. This is a valid fear. If we choose to follow God, we must count the cost.

HOW CAN I SPEAK IN TONGUES?

If you have been filled with the Holy Spirit and desire to speak in tongues, but are having trouble doing so, you may be asking, How can I overcome these obstacles? How can I be released in tongues?

First, you must examine your own heart. Do you really desire this gift? Or are there underlying fears and doubts that make you double-minded? (See Jas. 1:8.) If so, you need to confess these fears or doubts as sin.

The next step is simply to pray and wait on the Lord. Tell Him you desire His gifts. Ask Him to release the gift of tongues to you. It may also be helpful to have others pray for you.

If you are praying for the release of tongues, don't give up if the gift doesn't come right away. Remember, we are willing to ask repeatedly for that which we really want from God.

If you have prayed and still are not able to speak in tongues, the problem is probably that your mind is refusing to yield control of your voice to your spirit. One of the following techniques may be helpful in overcoming this obstacle.

TECHNIQUES FOR RELEASING TONGUES

Learning to operate in tongues is like learning to ride a bike. Almost anyone can ride a bike; any person with a minimal amount of coordination and balance can do it. Yet for those who have never tried it, there is some uncertainty about how to get started. There is a fear of lifting your feet from the ground, thrusting yourself forward and trusting in your sense of balance to keep you from falling. It usually takes a little experimenting to get the hang of it. Once you have done it, however, you never lose the ability.

Any Spirit-filled Christian has the capacity to speak in tongues, but for many there is still some uncertainty about how to get started. There is the fear of opening your mouth and beginning to speak when your mind is not supplying the content. For many, this takes a little experimenting. Once you have done it a few times, however, you can pray in tongues whenever you want to.

Several techniques can be helpful in overcoming these initial obstacles. Ideally, these techniques should not be necessary. If you have not been hindered in the release of tongues by some of the aforementioned fears, the release of tongues should be a very natural thing. If you have been hindered, however, the following techniques can be helpful as "training wheels" to get you started:

Technique #1

1. Pray for the gift of tongues to be released. It is helpful to have others lay hands on you and pray for you.
2. Begin to praise God verbally. Express your love and praise to Him.
3. At some point in your praise as you sense the presence of God, simply choose to stop speaking words your mind can understand. Choose to keep speaking, but determine not to say anything you understand. Simply allow your mouth to make sounds. This will break your mind's control over your vocal cords. At first, the sounds you make will seem forced. The first few sounds will probably not be tongues. They are simply the sounds you make when your mind is not allowed to provide the words. Within a few minutes, however, your spirit will take over, and tongues will begin to flow. This may be easier to do if you are whispering very quietly. The sound of your voice may be distracting to you at first.

Technique #2

Try to *sing* in tongues first. For some reason, it is easier for some people to begin by singing in tongues, perhaps because singing is associated with a different part of your brain. It can bypass some of your mind's defenses. At some point when you feel the Holy Spirit's presence, simply begin to sing praises to Him—either a song you know, or a "new song." At some point in the song, simply allow new words to flow. Continue this until you can *speak* in tongues, too.

Technique #3

Allow the Holy Spirit to filter His words through your mind at first. This can put your mind at ease. To do this, simply pray God would give you a few words in your tongue to pray to Him. God will usually respond by giving you a few strange-sounding words. When He does, simply choose to pray those words to Him over and over. Your tongues will soon be released and will begin to flow.

Remember, the technique is not crucial. I have known people who have been released in their tongues in each of these ways. As with riding a bike, the first time is the hardest. Once you have spoken in tongues a few times and know what it "feels" like to do it, you will be able to pray in tongues at will and on any occasion.

When you are released in the gift of tongues, remember that a gift will do you no good if you fail to use it. Pray in the Spirit on every occasion (see Eph. 6:18). Seek the Lord daily, and allow your spirit to express its deepest desires and highest praise to the Father.

REVELATION BY THE SPIRIT: AN INTRODUCTION TO THE PROPHETIC GIFTINGS

On September 21, 1994, while Chuck D. Pierce was ministering at a service in Houston, Texas, he gave the following prophetic word:

The next 24 days are critical! My eyes are upon this city and upon the remnant in this city, and I will overcome the structures that are set against My Spirit in this city! Revelation that has been withheld is going to begin to come down to people like rain. Look to the river on the east. As that river rises, so will my people! I see a fire. It is a literal fire! Fire is on the river. For the Lord says, "My fire will begin to come to this city!" I would call you to the night watch. Gather together in the night watch. If you will enter into the night watch, you will overthrow the impending destruction and doom that is set for the area.

When Chuck came back to Denton after that meeting, he told me of the prophecy and gave me the interpretation. He said that in 24 days God would send a flood to the river on the east side of

Houston, and there would be a fire on the river. This would picture in the natural realm what God was about to do in that city. But those who would enter into 24 days of prayer would escape the destruction that was to come.

In response to this prophetic word, Deborah DeGar, an intercessor from the Houston area, took the prophecy from church to church, leading a prayer watch from 3:00 A.M. to 6:00 A.M. for the next 24 days.

Twenty-four days later, the city of Houston was hit by one of the worst floods in its history. As the San Jacinto River east of the city flooded, some barges broke loose and careened down the flooded river, hitting and rupturing a natural gas pipeline. The gas erupted from beneath the river and ignited, creating an inferno of fire blazing in the very middle of the river.

I distinctly remember watching the news broadcast on network television and seeing footage of the fire blazing on the river east of the city, just as the prophet had predicted. This amazing event so quickened the faith of the churches involved that a fresh move of the Holy Spirit swept through the city.

It's significant to note that while many areas of the city were devastated by the floods, none of the churches that entered into prayer on the night watches suffered damage from the floods!

We live in a day when the Holy Spirit is being poured out on His people in a fresh and powerful way. In Acts 2:17,18 God promises, "In the last days...I will pour out My Spirit on all people. Your sons and daughters will *prophesy,* your young men will *see visions,* your old men will *dream dreams.* Even on my servants, both men and women I will pour out my Spirit in those days, and *they will prophesy*" (italics mine).

According to this passage, one of the results of the Holy Spirit's outpouring is the release of *prophetic gifting.* When men and women receive the Spirit's power, they are attuned to the voice of the Lord in a new way. They begin to hear prophetic words. They begin to have prophetic dreams. They begin to see visions. In both the Old and New Testaments, whenever the Holy Spirit "shows up," prophecy comes forth.

WHAT IS PROPHECY?

Prophecy is speaking forth the mind and heart of God as revealed by the Holy Spirit. Prophecy means *hearing* what God is saying and *communicating* that revelation to the Church in an appropriate time and manner.

Prophecy is an outflow of the heart and nature of God Himself. The God of the Bible is a God who communicates with His people. The prophets of the Old Testament ridiculed the pagans because they worshiped mute idols that could not speak to them. Jeremiah 10:5 compares this to bowing down before a scarecrow in a melon patch!

Some Christians question whether it's still possible to receive revelation from God, teaching instead that the gift of prophecy has ceased to function in the Church. The Bible, however, assures us that the gift of prophecy has not ceased. Paul wrote in 1 Corinthians 13:8-10 that prophecy will not cease until "that which is perfect has come" (NKJV).

I've heard some preachers claim the "perfect" is in fact the completed New Testament, but that idea is foreign to this passage. Paul goes on to tell us that when the perfect comes, we will see "face to face" and will know just as completely as we are known:

> Now we see but a poor reflection as in a mirror; then we shall see face to face. Now I know in part; then I shall know fully, even as I am fully known (1 Cor. 13:12).

Wayne Grudem, a professor at Trinity Evangelical Divinity School, points out that "face to face" is an Old Testament phrase for "seeing God personally" (see Gen. 32:30; Exod. 33:11; Deut. 5:4).[1] That can only be a reference to the second coming of Jesus. Grudem goes on to say that the phrase "then I shall know fully, even as I am fully known" must *also* refer to the Lord's return.[2]

Even the dispensational theologian Charles Ryrie, a former theology professor at Dallas Seminary, teaches that the "perfect" in this passage is a reference to Christ's second coming.[3] At the Second Coming, we will no longer need the gift of prophecy, for we will see Him face to face and shall know Him fully as we have been fully known. Until Jesus returns, however, the prophetic continues to be a vital line of communication between the Lord and His people.

The Bible assures us that it is not only *possible* to hear His voice, *it should be a common experience for every believer!* Jesus said, "My sheep hear my voice" (see John 10:14). If you are one of His sheep, you have the privilege of hearing His voice.

But God's Word is perfect! Isn't prophecy *adding* to the Bible? some Christians object. The answer is an emphatic NO!

Prophetic revelation is different from biblical revelation, falling under a different category altogether. Even in biblical times, the vast majority of prophetic words given were not considered to be part of the Scriptures. There are many, many prophets and prophetesses mentioned in the Bible who left behind no written record of the revelation they received.

Prophetic revelation is a "now" word. It's specific direction for a specific situation. Like manna, it's only for today. Scripture, on the other hand, is *eternal* truth; it applies in every situation.

Prophecy also differs from Scripture in its reliability. Prophetic revelation is given via a fallible human vessel. It is not complete (see 1 Cor. 13:9) and may be corrupted by the personality of the person who speaks it. For that reason, the Bible tells us that prophecy must always be *tested* (see 1 Cor. 14:29; 1 Thess. 5:21).

Scripture, however, is not only revealed by God, it is *inspired* by God (see 2 Tim. 3:16,17). Inspiration means that although God's truth was given through human personalities, it was supernaturally protected from contamination and error, so the words written in the original manuscripts of the Bible are *exactly* the words God intended. That's why we are never told to *test* Scripture. God assures us it is reliable.

Though nothing has been added to the Bible since the close of the first century, God continues to speak to us through His prophets. In every revival down through history, when the Holy Spirit was present, prophecy has taken place.

As I described in the introduction, the first time I knew I was hearing the voice of God was in October 1983. I was sitting at my desk on a Monday afternoon, studying. As I sat there reading the Bible, God spoke to me. He spoke only three brief statements, but His voice was so clear and penetrating I had no doubt it was Him. What He said was very significant to me, but more important was the fact I knew God had spoken to me. As He spoke, it broke a stronghold in my life.

Within two weeks of this incident I was baptized in the Holy Spirit and was speaking in tongues. From that point on, my wife and I found ourselves in a continual flow of revelation. We began having prophetic dreams. We began seeing visions. We began to receive prophetic words. All of those things we hadn't previously believed in suddenly started happening. I have now come to the point where I cannot imagine living the Christian life without the ability to hear from God.

WHY IS PROPHECY IMPORTANT?

Prophecy is important for several reasons:

Prophecy is important because God tells us it is important. God tells us we should seek to prophesy. "Desire earnestly spiritual gifts, but especially that you may prophesy" (1 Cor. 14:1, NASB). In the *King James Version*, 1 Corinthians 14:39 tells us to "covet" the gift of prophecy—the only thing in all the universe we are specifically told to covet!

What does it mean to covet something? When you covet something, you want it desperately. You think about it all the time. You desire it so much you constantly try to figure out how to get it. That's the attitude God wants us to have toward the gift of prophecy! God wants you to make it a high priority in your life to learn to operate in the prophetic.

Prophecy provides us direction from God. I grew up in a church that believed God had said everything worth saying by A.D. 95 and has been silent ever since—sort of a 2,000-year-old writer's block. For most of my Christian life, I was told the only source of revelation from God available to us today is the Bible. This worked well for issues the Bible spoke directly to. If I wanted to know if I should kill or steal, I could look in the Bible and get a clear answer.

In many other areas, however, just knowing the Book wasn't all that helpful. I was unable to find clear answers in the Word for questions like, Should I marry Susie or Jane? Should I move to Chicago or Detroit? or Should I take this job or that job?

The Bible makes it clear that God has a specific, detailed plan for my life. The choices I make matter to Him, but if God won't speak to me, I end up in a guessing game, trying to figure out what He wants me to do.

Over the years I've read many books on how to discern the will of God. These described all sorts of guidelines for wise decision-making, such as looking for biblical principles, seeking godly counsel, etc. By following these steps, you may be able to make a wise and well-informed decision, but there are still many times you will be left without much confidence that you know God's specific will for your life.

In the Bible, when God's people needed to discern His good will, they *asked* Him and He *told* them. God spoke to them and directed their steps through visions, dreams and prophetic words. Most pastors today would strongly discourage their church members from making a decision on the basis of a prophetic dream, yet that's one of the most common ways people in the Bible received direction from God. In the first two chapters of the New Testament alone, God gives direction through prophetic dreams *five times*! (See Matt. 1:20; 2:12, 13,19,22.)

People in the Bible never resorted to formulas for finding God's will! It wasn't through "seeking mature counsel" that Noah knew he was to build an ark. It wasn't by applying biblical principles that Hosea determined he was to marry a prostitute. It wasn't through his study of Scripture that Paul discovered his call as an apostle.

The God who spoke to men and women in biblical times has not changed. He still speaks to His children to give us direction and guidance.

Prophecy releases the life and the power of God. The voice of God not only communicates truth, it has power. It's living, active, sharper than any two-edged sword. Ezekiel saw the vision of the dry bones and heard God direct him to prophesy. The results were dramatic. As he was prophesying the bones came together, bone to bone, and tendon and flesh appeared. Breath entered into them and they came to life, and they stood on their feet, a mighty army (see Ezek. 37:7-10). When you prophesy, when the prophetic word of God goes forth, it doesn't just enlighten. It doesn't just give information. It releases *life*. It releases *power*. It *changes* situations.

Paul told Timothy that by following the prophetic words spoken over his life he would be enabled to fight the good fight, holding onto faith and a good conscience (see 1 Tim. 1:18,19). Some of you are in the fight. Even now you're in a battle, but God has released a prophetic word into your life. God wants you to know that by paying careful attention to that prophetic word you will receive the direction and the strength you need to stand in the day of battle.

If you have a prophetic word over your life, God wants you to take it seriously, to focus your attention on it so it can release a flow of faith into your life. Don't just write it down in the back of your Bible and never think of it again. As you focus on a prophetic word and pray over it, you will see God's strength, power and life released.

WALKING IN THE PROPHETIC

We must learn to walk in the prophetic as we learned to handle the Bible. In studying the Bible, there are definite steps we must follow if we want to receive the full benefit of God's Word. First, we must *receive* the message of the Bible into our hearts. We do this by reading it and studying it. Next, we must correctly *interpret* the Bible, so we can understand what it is saying. Finally, we must accurately *apply* the Bible, so we know how to obey it.

BENEFITING FROM THE BIBLE
RECEIVE IT → INTERPRET IT → APPLY IT

When we receive prophetic revelation, there are also steps we must follow to receive the full benefit of what God is saying. Because prophecy comes through fallible human beings, we must first *test* every prophetic word to be sure we have really heard from God. Then we must correctly *interpret* the message we have heard. Finally, we must accurately *apply* the prophetic word to discern how God wants us to respond to it.

BENEFITING FROM A PROPHETIC WORD
RECEIVE IT → TEST IT → INTERPRET IT → APPLY IT

TESTING PROPHETIC WORDS

As you become aware of the prophetic, you will find you live in a continual flow of revelation. It's like standing in the rain with revelation pouring down from on high. But "prophetic words" are not always what they seem. Sometimes you are hearing from God; at other times it's only your imagination (see Ezek. 13:17; Jer. 23:26). Some prophetic words may come from the enemy to bring deception (see Jer. 23:13; Isa. 47:13). Because of this, it's imperative to test prophetic words to discern what is from God and what is not (see 1 Cor. 14:29; 1 Thess. 5:20,21).

When I speak on the gift of prophecy, one of the most frequent questions I am asked is, How do I know if I'm really hearing God? Some of the books I recommend later in this chapter go into much more detail on the process of testing prophetic words. But here are a few basic guidelines for testing what you hear:

Test prophecy by the Bible. Does the word you hear contradict the Bible? God will not tell you one thing in His written Word, then say just the opposite in a prophetic word. Deuteronomy 13 warns us that even if a prophet gives an accurate prophecy, if he tries to lead you away from the truth of God, don't listen to him!

Test prophecy by the release of faith. Prophecy is the word of God, and the word of God releases faith. Faith comes by hearing and hearing comes from the word of God (see Rom. 10:17). When you hear a word from God, you will feel faith rising within you. It will stir your spirit. When you hear a word, pay attention to your spirit. Does that prophetic word produce faith?

Test prophecy through confirmation. When God gives you a word, He will not just say it once. He will usually repeat it over and over to you in a variety of ways. In your Bible reading, verses that confirm the word will "jump off the page." You may have dreams and visions. Prophetic words will be given to you by others to confirm what God has spoken to you personally.

Several weeks ago, a young woman named Rhonda visited our church. I had met Rhonda on several occasions, but I knew very little about her, other than that she worked with a large missions organization. When she was introduced to the congregation that morning, God gave me a vision. In my spirit, I saw a set of keys. It was just a momentary picture that flashed in my mind, but I sensed what God was saying.

Later in the service, I gave Rhonda a prophetic word that went something like this: "God has placed you in a key position. You have wondered many times why He has placed you in that position, and you have even questioned whether you have the ability to do what you are called to do. God would say to you, 'I have given you the *keys* to open many doors. Move forward in faith, and I will use you to open many doors for My Church.'"

As I spoke that word, I could tell by Rhonda's response that it was a significant word to her. In fact, when I spoke the word "keys" she almost fell over! After the service, Rhonda explained that the previous week a prophet in a different church had given her the same word. All week she had been praying about that prophecy and had spent several hours in prayer the night before asking God to give her revelation about the keys.

While my prophetic word did not *add* anything to what Rhonda had already heard, it served as a strong *confirmation* of what God was saying over her life! When God speaks a word over your life, you can expect it to be confirmed again and again.

Test prophecy by the witness of godly leaders. Another way to test revelation is by the witness of others who hear from God (see Matt. 18:16). Do recognized prophets agree with what you've heard? This is particularly important if you are just beginning to hear God. Let's suppose you get a word that says, "I want you to quit your job and move to another city." That *could* be God, but with a decision that important, I'd suggest you get confirmation. Go to people in leadership who know you and who have a reputation for hearing God. Ask them, "Does this bear witness?" They will be able to discern the voice of God if God has spoken. God's word will bear witness in their spirits.

If you receive a word that passes all four of these tests, you can be fairly confident that you have received a word from God.

INTERPRETING PROPHECY

Prophecy frequently must be interpreted, as often the message is veiled in symbolism. Once when God gave Jeremiah a vision, He asked, "Jeremiah, what do you see?"

Jeremiah answered, "I see two baskets with figs in them. One of them has good figs and one of them has bad figs" (see Jer. 24:1,2).

God wants you to know what His prophetic word means. If you seek Him, He will give you the interpretation.

If God gave you a vision of two baskets full of figs, what would you think? You might say, "That can't be God! Why would God give me a vision of figs!" But this vision was from God, and it was vitally important for Jeremiah to learn what those figs signified.

God is infinitely creative, and He sometimes selects unusual ways of communicating His truth to His people. Here are some general principles for interpreting prophecy:

Ask God for the interpretation. All interpretation ultimately comes from God. How did Jeremiah find out what those two baskets of figs meant? He didn't go around asking his friends, "What do you think figs symbolize?" He went directly to the Lord, and God *told* him what the figs meant.

Daniel had a vision he did not understand so he prayed and fasted for 21 days until, finally, an angel came and gave him the interpretation (see Dan. 10). God wants you to know what His prophetic word means. If you seek Him, He will give you the interpretation.

Gain interpretation through the Word. This is a particularly important step if the message contains types and symbols. Many of the common prophetic pictures and symbols are explained in the Bible. Go to the Word and fill your mind with the Word, and you will begin to understand what those symbols mean.

Gain interpretation from the context. Many times you'll get an interpretation from the *context* of what God is doing in your life. When our church was beginning to transition toward the things of the Spirit, we went through some difficult days. In the midst of this, God gave my wife, Linda, a prophetic dream. In the dream, Linda gave birth to a baby, but the baby was premature. It was tiny, about the size of a man's thumb, and she thought it was going to die. As she watched, however, the baby became plump and grew healthy. When Linda woke up, God said to her, "That's the church. It was born too soon, but it's going to be fine." For the next several years, at crucial points in the church's history, she had prophetic dreams about a baby. In the context, she didn't have to wonder what the baby meant. We knew God was giving further revelation about the church.

Gain interpretation through gifted people. In the book of Genesis, Pharaoh, the pagan king of Egypt, had a prophetic dream. Pharaoh's advisors were unable to provide an interpretation, so he turned to Joseph who told him what it meant. In Daniel 2, Nebuchadnezzar, the pagan king of Babylon, had a prophetic dream. His wise men couldn't tell him what it meant.

He went to Daniel who said, "Let me pray about it overnight, and God will tell me what it means." Daniel got the interpretation.

These passages reveal a basic biblical principle: If you can't interpret a prophetic word, go to someone who can. Go to those who have the gift of interpretation and let them seek the Lord with you for the meaning.

God wants you to care enough to gain an understanding of what He has said. If God speaks to you, don't just put it on the shelf. Begin to pray and seek the Lord. That word may be exactly what you're going to need in the days ahead. God will often reveal His will in a way that is hard to understand because He desires you to search for it. He wants you to develop a hunger for understanding His ways and His words.

APPLYING PROPHECY

When you receive revelation from the Lord, it's important to know what it means, but it's just as important to know what you are supposed to do with it. You need to discern *why* God has given this revelation to you.

When some people get a prophetic word for another person, they feel the need to run right out and tell that person what God is saying to him or her. Sometimes that's what you're supposed to do. But sometimes that's the *worst* thing you can do. I've seen Chuck Pierce hold a prophetic word for years before he felt at liberty to release it to the affected individuals. Don't give a prophetic word until it is the right time and the right place.

In trying to discern what to do with a prophetic word, it's helpful to remember why prophetic words are given. The purpose of prophetic gifting is most clearly summed up in 1 Corinthians 14:3: "But everyone who prophesies speaks to men for their *strengthening, encouragement* and *comfort*" (italics added). If God gives you a prophetic word, it is given to accomplish at least one of these three things:

183

1. To strengthen someone in the Lord by releasing new faith and vision.
2. To encourage someone in their call, motivating them to press on into the destiny God has for them.
3. To comfort those who are wounded by releasing a new awareness of God's love and power.

A person who holds the *office* of prophet has authority to go beyond these spheres, but basic, "everyday" prophecy has these clear boundaries.

A prophetic word that is not given in God's time and in God's way can bring much harm. When our church was just beginning to move in the gift of prophecy, a woman in our church received a prophetic word for me. It was at a time when the church was going through a difficult transition and I was exhausted—physically, emotionally and spiritually. We had just gotten over a major hurdle, and I was looking forward to a season of R & R before facing another battle.

This woman came to me and said, "God says He's going to put you through a really hard time. It's going to be a lot worse than anything you've ever gone through. It's going to shake your faith! After you're through this, God will bring you out into a place of blessing."

I was devastated by that word! I wanted to say, "Get thee behind me, Satan!" I was so exhausted from the battle I had been through, I was not encouraged by the message of blessing at the end. I didn't think I could face another season of warfare. I talked to my wife for some encouragement and she said, "I think that's a word from God."

Dealing with that prophetic word was one of the most difficult trials I've ever faced. It almost shook my faith in the goodness of God. Given at that time, that word did not strengthen. It did not encourage. It did not comfort. It didn't help at all!

But it was a true word. It came true exactly as prophesied,

but knowing about that difficult season ahead of time did not make it easier. It made it harder. What was the problem?

I'm convinced the woman did hear God, but in her inexperience she did not take the extra step to ask God what to do with the word she had received. What she should have done is this:

When she heard from God what I was about to go through, she should have gone into *intercession* for me. Many times when God gives you a prophetic word, His purpose is not for you to tell someone else, but to direct you in prayer. This woman should have held on to that word, waited with it, and prayed for me until she saw I was right in the middle of the testing.

Then she could have come to me and told me, "God told me two months ago that you were going to go through this and He's had me praying for you. God told me that He is going to bring you through this trial and bring you out into a time of great blessing!" That would have lifted my spirit! It would have *encouraged* me to know that she had already been praying for me. It would have *comforted* me to know that a time of great blessing lay ahead. It would have *strengthened* me to press on in the battle!

The way and the time a word is communicated can make all the difference. When you have a prophetic word, don't just blurt it out. Seek the Lord's direction for that word. "Lord, how do you want this used? When do you want this released?" Release it at a time when it will accomplish God's purposes.

LEARNING TO HEAR
THE VOICE OF GOD

How do you learn to hear the voice of God? Here are some basic steps in learning to recognize the voice of the Holy Spirit:

Be filled with the Spirit. You don't *have* to be baptized in the Holy Spirit to receive a prophetic word. You don't even have to be saved to receive prophecy. Nebuchadnezzar was a pagan, yet he received one of the greatest prophetic dreams in the Bible. Numbers 22 shows that God can even speak through a donkey!

Yet prophecy is connected with the Spirit's empowering ministry. The empowering of the Holy Spirit sensitizes you to hear and recognize what the Spirit is saying. If you desire to hear God more clearly, the first step is to seek His empowering.

Recognize that God is speaking to you. Don't ever say, "I can't hear God!" To say that is to call Jesus a liar, for He said, "My sheep hear my voice" (see John 10:14). God says you *can* hear His voice. God says prophecy *is* for you (see 1 Cor. 14:31).

First Corinthians 2:16 tells us that as believers, we have the mind of Christ. If you know Jesus as your Savior, you have the source of prophetic revelation dwelling in your heart right now. The Holy Spirit is in continual communion with your spirit. He's pouring His word through you. Your spirit is continually flooded with His revelation. He's expressing Himself to you, and you can discern His voice and exercise the gift of prophecy.

All kinds of people can prophesy—young and old, men and women, slaves and free. Whatever your station in life, whatever your gender, whatever your age, if you have the Holy Spirit, you can hear God (see Acts 2:17,18). Draw close to Him and realize that He is speaking to you.

Make it your goal *to hear the voice of God.* Learning to prophesy requires effort. God's Word tells us to covet the gift of prophecy (see 1 Cor. 14:39, *KJV*). This calls for action on your part. Pursue it, seek it, make it a conscious goal in your life to learn to prophesy. The Bible also indicates that training and instruction in the prophetic is beneficial. Elijah founded schools at Gilgal and Bethel to train up new prophets.[4] (See 2 Kings 2:2.)

One way to pursue this goal is to read books that will help you develop this gift. In recent years, a number of excellent books have been written on the subject of the prophetic. Two of my favorites are Cindy Jacobs's *The Voice of God* (Regal Books) and Graham Cook's *Developing Your Prophetic Gifting* (Renew

Books). Both provide valuable insight into developing and exercising the prophetic gifts.

Another way to grow in prophecy is through attending prophetic conferences. I have greatly benefited from workshops with prophets like Chuck D. Pierce, Barbara Wentroble, Barbara Yoder and Jim Stephens. Seek opportunities to be trained and nurtured in the prophetic gifts!

Learn how God speaks. How do we hear God's voice? Sometimes God speaks in an audible voice, but that is rare. More commonly, He will speak into your mind in a voice you know did not come from you. Sometimes He will speak through a verse of Scripture that just "jumps off the page" as you read it, and you will know that God is speaking that verse into a specific situation in your life. Sometimes He will speak to you through a dream. Sometimes a mental picture will flash into your mind. Sometimes you will just "know." Make it your goal to hear Him in whatever form He chooses to communicate.

Fill your mind with the Word. The most effective prophets I've known have been people who have spent great amounts of time in the Bible. The written Word of God sensitizes your mind to hear the thoughts of God when He speaks prophetically.

Pray in the Spirit. Praying in tongues strengthens your inner man and sensitizes your spirit to receive revelation from God. When I need to hear God, I often begin by praying in tongues. It opens a door for prophetic revelation to flow, and I am soon able to discern what God is saying.

Ask God the right questions, and obey Him when He answers. If you want to receive revelation from God, begin by asking Him the right questions. There are some questions God will always answer. Ask God, "Who do you want me to pray for?" As you begin your daily time with the Lord, lean back, relax and ask God to bring to mind those people He wants you to pray for. God will begin, one by one, to show you those He wants you to remember in prayer. You may be surprised. He may bring to mind people you haven't thought of for years. He may impress you to pray for specific things for some of these people. Prayer is one of the key avenues for learning to hear God.

Another question God will always answer is "What sins do you want me to confess?" Get out a sheet of paper and pray as David did: "Lord, search me!" Ask God to search your heart and reveal areas of sin He wants you to deal with; then be quiet and allow Him to bring them to your mind. As He reveals areas of sin, write down everything He shows you; then confess and repent, claiming His forgiveness as promised in 1 John 1:9. If you've had a hard time hearing God, I guarantee this will work. You'll be surprised how much He says to you! As you confess the sins He shows you, thank Him that you are forgiven by the blood of Jesus. As you do this, you will find a whole new openness and freedom in your communication with God.

And when an offering is about to be taken, don't just pull a few dollars out of your wallet. Ask God, "What do you want me to give?" God never fails to answer this one, and again, you may be surprised by what He says. If you determine to obey Him, you will see Him release great blessing in your life.

A SAFEGUARD FOR BEGINNERS

As you learn to hear the voice of God, it's important to remember that prophecy must always take place *under authority*. First Chronicles 25:2 talks about men who prophesied under Asaph's supervision, and Asaph prophesied under the king's supervision. God has established an authority structure. Just because you're prophesying doesn't mean that you're suddenly directing everything. Don't go to your pastor and expect him to obey you because you've "heard from God"! Prophecy flows under authority.

Also, a prophet must always prophesy with humility. Desire to see your word tested. Some people get offended if someone wants to test their word or question something they have said. God wants us to learn to prophesy with humility. Realize you might not be hearing everything you think you're hearing. First Corinthians 13:9 says we prophesy in part. Your prophetic word may be incomplete. Your understanding of it may also be incomplete. You may not have understood God's timing or the process involved in walking through a prophetic word.

If you are a beginner, submit your word to more experienced believers for evaluation. Allow your leaders to speak into your life and give you correction, direction and encouragement as you are learning to prophesy. If you are willing to walk in humility and receive correction, God will sharpen your gift and allow you to minister with great effectiveness.

THE GIFTS OF HEALING

It was the spring of 1970, and I was in my senior year at the University of South Florida. One Thursday evening I began to experience a persistent pain and pressure in my left side. As this pain increased, it became so severe that I finally made my way to the campus infirmary, where my problem was diagnosed as a kidney stone.

If you've never had a kidney stone, you won't appreciate this, but a kidney stone is one of the most painful infirmities you can have. I've been told it's the only pain a man can experience that compares with the pain of childbirth.

They gave me the strongest painkillers they had at the campus infirmary, but as the hours went by, the pain was so intense I couldn't sleep. So I got out a pocket New Testament and began to read the Gospel of Mark. As I read, the Spirit of God touched my heart. The passage read, "And a leper came to Him, beseeching Him and falling on his knees before Him, and saying to Him, 'If You are willing, You can make me clean.' And moved with compassion, [Jesus] stretched out His hand, and touched him, and said to him, 'I am willing; be cleansed.' And immediately the leprosy left him and he was cleansed" (Mark 1:40-42, NASB).

As I read that, it occurred to me that if I could go back in time to A.D. 28 and stand before Jesus and ask Him for healing, He would heal me! I had no doubt about that. Jesus never refused anyone who came to Him for healing.

Then the Lord reminded me of Jesus' promise: "I am with you

always" (Matt. 28:20). Even though Jesus was not visibly present, through His Holy Spirit His presence was just as real in that infirmary as it was in the days of the apostles.

So why couldn't I ask Him for healing and be healed? Almost without thinking, as I lay there in excruciating pain, I said, "Lord! If You are willing, You can heal me!"

Immediately the answer came back, "I am willing! Be healed!" As I heard those words in my spirit, it was like someone flipped a switch, and the pain stopped. It wasn't a gradual reduction. The pain stopped instantaneously and did not return. I soon went to sleep and was dismissed from the infirmary the next morning.

That was my first encounter with divine healing. I knew that God had supernaturally healed me, but I was in a theological environment where testimonies of healing were not greatly emphasized. While I was thankful for my healing, I assumed it was one of those wonderful exceptions to the rule. My thinking went something like this: Though God is not *generally* interested in healing the sick, He was gracious to me and answered my prayer. During the ensuing years of theological study, the incident was nearly forgotten. It was not until almost ten years later, through the ministry of Pat Jarrard, that God would again focus my attention on the reality of divine healing.

The ministry of healing is inseparably linked to the power of the Holy Spirit. Wherever the Spirit's power is embraced, miraculous healing takes place. No teaching on the Holy Spirit can be complete without understanding His power in healing.

WHAT IS HEALING?

John Wimber defined healing as a noticeable improvement in physical condition in response to the prayer of faith. That's a good definition, but it's not complete. Healing includes more than just physical improvement. The biblical words for healing describe a *restoration* to wholeness. Healing means being restored to God's created design and purpose in *every* area of life.

While we usually think of healing in terms of physical restoration, healing also includes emotional and spiritual restoration. The Bible teaches that God desires to restore us to wholeness in our bodies (see Exod. 23:25; Deut. 7:15; Jas. 5:15), our emotions (see Ps. 147:3; Isa. 61:1-3) and our spirits (see Jer. 3:22; Hos. 14:4).

Many people today have developed misconceptions about divine healing. Some think if healing is from God, it's always instantaneous. The Bible, however, shows that healing is not always immediate. Sometimes it is a *process*. Jesus said that His followers "will lay hands on the sick, and they will *recover*" (Mark 16:18, *NASB*, italics mine). This verse pictures a sick person whose condition is not improving. When a believer lays hands on the sick and prays for their healing, however, the power of sickness is broken and rapid recovery begins.

This is a common response to healing prayer. In my ministry, instantaneous healing has been rare, but I have *often* seen prayer break the power of infirmity and bring overnight recovery. Last year, a group from our church was asked to go and pray for a woman in the hospital. This woman was having circulation problems and was to have her foot amputated the next morning. When we entered the room and uncovered her foot, we were shocked. It looked like the foot was already dead. Its color was black, the skin hard, stiff and cold. As we poured oil over the foot and prayed, we sensed a strong flow of anointing, but there was no immediate visible change in the foot. By the time the doctors came in the next morning, however, the foot had regained its normal color. One of the doctors declared, "This foot doesn't need to be amputated, it has *life* in it!" A few days later, the woman was released from the hospital with both feet intact, and she has experienced no further problems.

Sometimes healing is only partial, or it may come in stages. When Jesus ministered to the blind man in Mark 8:23-25 there was, at first, a *partial* healing. The man gained sight, but not with clarity. He saw men as "trees walking." Then Jesus touched him again and the healing process was completed.

Another misconception about divine healing is that divine healing is always permanent. The Bible teaches that just the opposite is true! If the underlying problems are not dealt with, infirmity can indeed return. In John 5:14, Jesus warns a man he has healed, "Sin no more, lest a worse thing come upon you" (*NKJV*). In Matthew 12:45, Jesus indicates that a person suffering as a result of demonic oppression may experience a return of the problem—and worse—if precautions are not taken.

Another all-too-common misconception about healing concerns medical treatment. Some who believe in divine healing think it's a sin to go to a doctor. That's a false assumption. Jesus Himself said that sick people need a physician (see Luke 5:31). A belief in divine healing does not rule out medical treatment.

REQUIREMENTS FOR HEALING

For healing to take place, or for any ministry to be effective for that matter, we must come equipped with two basic tools:

1. *We must have the anointing of God.* If you want to minister healing, you must be empowered by the Holy Spirit. As we have seen, even Jesus did not attempt to minister until the power of the Holy Spirit came upon Him. Jesus cautioned His followers not to begin their ministry until they were "clothed in power from on high" (Luke 24:49).

Only the anointing will produce effective ministry. Some try to minister to the sick with a display of emotion. They weep and cry and hug all over sick people. But all the compassion in the world will not make the sick well.

Others attempt to minister through the intellect. They try to give the suffering person a better understanding of his problem. I've seen pastors sit with people confined to a hospital bed and say, "What is God teaching you through this?" But Jesus didn't try to help people *understand* their sickness. He just healed them!

Ministry does not happen by way of our intellect or emotions. Nor will the sick be healed by sheer force of will. Healing comes through a release of the power of the Holy Spirit. If you are filled with the Spirit, that power to heal is within you *now*.

2. *We must have faith.* The New Testament shows that faith *releases* the Spirit's anointing to operate in a situation. On many occasions, Jesus commended those who received healing by saying, "Your faith has made you well" (see Matt. 9:22; Mark 5:34; Luke 8:48). Their faith released the anointing so healing could occur.

The reverse is also true. *Unbelief hinders the anointing so healing cannot operate.* In Matthew 17:15-20, the disciples asked Jesus why they were unable to heal a boy with seizures. Jesus answered them, "Because you have so little faith." When Jesus visited His hometown, there was such an atmosphere of unbelief that His anointing could not operate. Matthew 13:58 says, "He did not do many miracles there because of their lack of faith." Mark 6:5,6 puts it in even stronger terms: "He *could not* do any miracles there, except lay his hands on a few sick people and heal them. And he was amazed at their lack of faith" (italics mine). *Where the general attitude toward divine healing was skepticism and unbelief, even Jesus could not heal!*

That's the tragic situation in many churches today, where Christians are not taught to trust God for healing. If the subject of healing comes up at all, the focus of the teaching is on why we should *not expect* God to heal us.

One of the professors I most admired at Dallas Theological Seminary was Dr. John F. Walvoord. Dr. Walvoord is a man with a heart for God and a genuine love for the Word. He is the former president of Dallas Seminary and a highly respected theologian in much of the evangelical church. In preparing to write this chapter, I picked up his book *The Holy Spirit*. What I discovered reflects much of the modern church's attitude toward healing.

Dr. Walvoord has written 288 pages on the ministry of the Holy Spirit, yet he devotes but *one paragraph* to the subject of healing. In that paragraph, he asserts *four times* that the gift of healing is *not* for today. He writes that the gift of healing has "ceased as a gift," that it "is no longer bestowed," that it "is not now committed unto men" and that "no one today" has this gift.[1]

Dr. Walvoord is by no means alone in his point of view. Much of the Church teaches that God is simply not interested in healing the sick, so it's not surprising that Christians today have very little expectation that He will heal them, their neighbors and their loved ones.

HEALING AND THE WILL OF GOD

For us to have the necessary faith for healing to take place, we must recognize that it *is* God's will to heal the sick. There is a great deal of biblical evidence to support this position.

The Bible shows that healing is God's nature. Throughout the Old Testament, the Lord revealed Himself to His people by a series of compound names. These names were made up of the name *Jehovah* (YHWH)—usually translated "Lord"—followed by a word that describes one aspect of His nature. A few of these compound names are:

Jehovah Jireh—the Lord Who Sees and Provides (Gen. 22:14)

Jehovah Nissi—the Lord Our Banner of Victory (Exod.
17:15)
Jehovah Tsidkenu—the Lord Our Righteousness (Jer. 23:5,6)
Jehovah Rohi—the Lord My Shepherd (Ps. 23:1)
Jehovah Shammah—the Lord Who Is Present (Exod. 40:35)

Taken together, these names present a portrait of the nature of God. He is a God who is always present, who sees our needs and meets them, who leads us in His victory.

One of these Old Testament compound names, *Jehovah Rapha*, is found in Exodus 15:26 where it is translated "I am the Lord, who heals you."

The Hebrew word *rapha* means to cure, mend and repair. In identifying Himself by this name, God has revealed that it's part of His nature to restore and bring to wholeness. He is a God who binds up the brokenhearted, strengthens the weak and heals those who are sick and wounded (see Isa. 61:1; Mal. 4:2). The desire to heal is part of God's very nature.

*It is indeed the will of the Father that we
be healed. In all of His earthly ministry,
Jesus never refused to heal anyone who
asked for healing.*

The Bible shows that healing is God's promise. Healing is not only part of God's nature, it is part of His promise to us. Throughout the Bible, God promises physical healing to His people (see Exod. 23:25; Deut. 7:15; Isa. 53:4,5; Jas. 5:15). In Psalm 103:3, for example, God links the *forgiving of all sin* and the *healing of all diseases*, identifying these as two of the benefits of knowing the Lord.

The Bible shows that healing is the Father's will. The New Testament tells us that Jesus was the perfect expression of the Father's will (see John 1:18). Jesus is quoted as saying, "It is written about me in the scroll—I have come to do your will, O God" (Heb. 10:7). If you want to know what the Father's will is, simply look at Jesus and His ministry.

So what did Jesus do when people came to Him for healing? He *healed* them! The leper *did not know* if it was God's will to heal, so Jesus assured him, "I am willing! Be healed!" (see Mark 1:41).

The ministry of Jesus shows that it is indeed the will of the Father that we be healed. In all of His earthly ministry, Jesus never refused to heal anyone who asked for healing. In fact, the Gospels show that one of Jesus' *primary* activities was the healing of the sick. Some have estimated that Jesus devoted more than one-half His ministry to healing those with physical infirmities.

Consider the following verses (italics added) and let the Spirit of God stir faith in your heart for healing:

People brought to him all who were ill with various diseases, those suffering severe pain, the demon-possessed, those having seizures, and the paralyzed, and he *healed* them (Matt. 4:24).

When evening came, many who were demon-possessed were brought to him, and he drove out the spirits with a word and *healed* all the sick (Matt. 8:16).

Many followed him, and he *healed* all their sick (Matt. 12:15).

They brought him a demon-possessed man who was blind

and mute, and Jesus *healed* him, so that he could both talk and see (Matt. 12:22).

When Jesus landed and saw a large crowd, he had compassion on them and *healed* their sick (Matt. 14:14).

All who touched him were *healed* (Matt. 14:36).

Great crowds came to him, bringing the lame, the blind, the crippled, the mute and many others, and laid them at his feet; and he *healed* them (Matt. 15:30).

Large crowds followed him, and he *healed* them there (Matt. 19:2).

The blind and the lame came to him at the temple, and he *healed* them (Matt. 21:14).

When the sun was setting, the people brought to Jesus all who had various kinds of sickness, and laying his hands on each one, he *healed* them (Luke 4:40).

Jesus said to Jairus, "Don't be afraid; just believe, and she will be *healed*" (Luke 8:50).

Jesus not only healed all who came to Him, He taught His followers to continue His healing ministry (see Mark 16:18; Luke 9:1,2,6; Luke 10:8,9; John 14:12).

Jesus was and is the great physician. He cares, not only for broken hearts, but for broken bodies. He desires to heal spiritually and physically. He healed the sick during His earthly ministry, and He has not changed. He is "the same yesterday and today and forever" (Heb. 13:8). His life and ministry reveal that it is God's will to heal!

THE REALITY OF HEALING TODAY

Do miraculous healings still take place as they did in the Bible? If you are in a church that prays for the sick, that may seem like a silly question, but for many it is a question of vital importance.

When I was in the evangelical movement, I seriously doubted that God was still in the healing business. Because I accepted a theology that taught against divine healing, I assumed that all claims of healing were bogus. When I would see someone on television give testimony to God's healing, I would secretly wonder if they had been paid to lie, just to make the evangelist look good.

In recent years, God has shown me that the large, well-known healing ministries are just a small part of what the Holy Spirit is doing in the area of healing. Most healing takes place at home and in one-on-one ministry encounters through average, everyday Christians who have learned to trust God for healing. Since the days when Pat Jarrard came and prayed for our children, I have found that supernatural, miraculous healing is far more common—and readily available—than most Christians ever imagine.

The first time I taught on healing in our church was early in our transitional phase, as our church was discovering the power of the Holy Spirit. I had seen God perform amazing healings in my own family, but there had not yet been much in the way of divine healing in our church.

One day as I was driving down the street, my heart was burdened about the number of people in the church with physical illness. I cried out to the Lord, "Lord! You need to teach them about healing!"

Without hesitation, the Lord answered back very firmly, "*You* teach them!"

After some hesitation, I taught a two-week series on healing. I concluded the second message with a low-key invitation. Having never held a healing service before, and not quite sure if God would *really* heal anyone, I simply asked those who wanted prayer for healing to raise their hands. Other members of the congregation were instructed to reach out and put a hand on a nearby individual's shoulder and quietly pray for God to heal that person.

And God worked! Five different people came to me that week to tell me that God had healed them. One woman was scheduled to go into the hospital Monday morning for a hysterectomy. When she arrived at the hospital, the doctor examined her, told her she no longer needed surgery and sent her home! Despite my inexperience and unbelief, God had *healed*.

The next few weeks, however, were a time of real turmoil in the church. Many people were upset that we had prayed for the sick! The wife of one of our deacons called my wife and told her, "When Robert taught about healing, I could see it was in the Bible. But when we actually prayed for the sick, it made me very uncomfortable. We can't stay in a church where that kind of thing happens."

Several families actually *left the church* because we prayed for God to heal sick people! One of our key leaders told me point-blank, "I don't want to be in a healing church."

I was amazed! Jesus spent more than half his time healing the sick; yet here were people who claimed to love Jesus, but they refused to stay in a church where the sick got healed.

This incident revealed to me two facts that I've since found to be consistently true. First, *God is much more willing to heal than we imagine.* I don't think we've ever had a time of prayer for the sick in our services without someone getting healed.

The second truth I learned from this encounter is that *churches are much less willing to pray for the sick* than I would have imagined. Praying for the sick moves a church out of its comfort zone, out of "safe" territory where the Holy Spirit's power can be intellectually debated. When the power of the Spirit is openly manifested, a church moves beyond the boundaries of theological discussion and comes face to face with the reality of the spiritual realm.

HOW TO PRAY FOR THE SICK

Praying for the sick is a ministry close to the heart of Jesus. It is an earthly demonstration of His power, His authority, His love and compassion.

As you pray for the sick, I recommend praying with open eyes and a sensitive spirit. There are many approaches to prayer for healing. I have adapted the following guidelines from a teaching by John Wimber that has proven to be very helpful.

1. *Ask the person where it hurts.* When you have opportunity to pray for healing, begin by asking "Where does it hurt?" You don't need a medical diagnosis of the problem, but it's good to have a basic idea of what you are praying for. Generally speaking, the more specifically you can pray, the more effective your prayer will be.

2. *Ask God for direction in how to pray.* Sickness can result from an interplay of a number of factors. On the natural level, physical problems can result from injury, from infection, from a genetic disorder or simply from physical weakness caused by inactivity, a lack of sleep or an improper diet. Sickness often has an emotional component. Emotional stress, depression, anger, fear and worry can all produce physical symptoms. Infirmity may also have a spiritual component, originating from sin, a curse, demonic oppression or simply as an attack from the enemy. Because so many factors may be involved, it's always a good idea to get direction from God on how to pray.

Jesus dealt with physical problems in a number of ways:

Sometimes He simply placed His hands on the sick person.

Sometimes He cast out a demon.

Sometimes He pronounced the person healed.

Sometimes He forgave the person's sins.

Sometimes He simply spoke to the problem.

Sometimes He performed a prophetic act, like putting mud on a person's eyes.

Sometimes He gave the person an assignment to carry out.

The only methodology Jesus followed was to be sensitive to the Father and do what the Father directed Him to do. As you speak with the person in need of healing, be sensitive to the leading of the Lord. Allow God to speak to you and give you insight into the problem and the kind of prayer necessary to bring about healing.

3. *Lay hands on the person and begin to pray.* If God has given you instruction on how to pray, follow it. If you haven't received specific direction, simply lay hands on the individual and pray for God to heal. It's not necessary to put your hands directly on the problem area. It's often best to lay hands on the person's head or shoulders.

When praying for the sick, it's sometimes helpful to minister with others as a team. When the gift of healing is mentioned in 1 Corinthians 12, the Greek words for "gift" and "healing" are both plural. There are "gifts of healings." To bring healing may require several gifts to be in operation at the same time. A word of knowledge may provide insight into the root problem. The gift of miracles may be necessary to restore damage done by an injury. Some people seem to have the gift of faith to trust God to break the power of specific kinds of infirmities. I've found that ministering as a group with several gifts in operation greatly increases the effectiveness of the prayer.

4. *Be alert to evidence that God is working.* When you pray for the sick, it's not necessary for you to feel anything. There may

be no outward evidence, yet healing can be taking place. Healing does not always require prolonged prayer, either. Sometimes a very brief prayer produces great results.

At other times, however, there is specific evidence that God is at work. You may feel heat or energy in your hands as you pray. You may see physical changes taking place in the person you are praying for. That's why I suggest you pray with your eyes open.

If you see evidence that the Holy Spirit is doing something, keep praying. If you're not sure, ask the person what they are feeling. When you sense that God is in the process of healing, I've found it's helpful to continue in prayer until one of the following takes place:

- Nothing more seems to be happening.
- The person is healed.
- You sense that it's time to stop.
- The person indicates he or she is ready for you to stop.

5. *Leave the results in God's hands.* Don't be overly concerned about whether the person has been immediately healed. Divine healing may take several hours to become evident. In any event, healing is *God's* job. Your job is to minister in the power of the Spirit as the Lord directs. Do what God has given you to do and leave the results with Him.

God is calling His Church to continue His ministry of healing. He is looking for a people who will not just *talk* about His love and power, but who will actively *demonstrate* His love and power on the earth in tangible ways. He desires a Bride who will express His heart through effective ministry to the sick and suffering, demonstrating—as He did—that the kingdom of God is at hand.

The Manifest Presence
of the Spirit

Dan enjoyed his walks along the river. Though he was far from home, separated from his friends and family, there was something about the quiet water of the great river that gave him a peaceful feeling. Sometimes he would walk alone for hours, praying and meditating on the Word.

As he walked along the grassy bank this day, however, he was not alone. Several men from the government office where he worked had joined him for an afternoon stroll. As they walked together, they talked about the affairs of state, about the political situation, about the perennial threat of war.

As they neared the bend of the river on the outskirts of the city, Dan felt a strange physical sensation. The air seemed to thicken. He felt weak and found himself struggling for a breath. His whole body began to tremble as waves of heat rolled over him.

At first, he thought he might be coming down with the flu, but it was clear the men with him were experiencing the same sensations. His associates exchanged terrified glances and cried out, "Do you feel that? What is that? I...I'm getting out of here!" In an almost comical display, they turned and stumbled through the mud into the tall reeds beside the river.

In the midst of the phenomenon, however, Dan felt a strange sense of peace. After the initial surprise, he sensed the familiar presence of the Holy Spirit around him. He began to feel weaker and his knees trembled.

Looking up, he saw what appeared to be an angel, clothed in golden light, speaking to him. Before he could hear what the angel was saying, however, he was overwhelmed by the mighty presence of God. His face turned pale, and he fell to the ground, unconscious.

How did you respond to the story you just read?

You may have felt it was a little too strange. After all, you've never experienced anything like that. You may be a little skeptical, saying to yourself, *That doesn't sound like God to me! If I experienced something like that, I'd say it was a demon!*

Or you may have experienced some things that while not identical, were similar enough that you can relate to this experience. You may be thinking, *Maybe that really was God. I've felt strange sensations like that when I was in the presence of God.*

Or you may have recognized immediately that Dan's experience was, in fact, a real encounter with the God of the Bible. You have full confidence Dan was in the presence of God, because you recognized this was not a contemporary story. You recognized it as the experience of the prophet Daniel as recorded in the Word of God! (See Daniel 10:4-11.)

Sadly, many Christians today are unfamiliar with the manifest presence of God. They have had little personal experience with God, and have not taken the time to study through the Bible to see how God's Word describes such an experience. So when they hear an account of someone else's experience with God, they are quick to judge it on the basis of their own experience—or lack thereof—and condemn that experience as false.

The Bible teaches, however, that our God manifests Himself tangibly to His people. He comes to them to heal, empower and refresh. God doesn't want you to just *know about* Him. He wants you to *experience* Him! He wants to manifest His presence in your life.

Let's examine some practical truths that will help you to experience the manifest presence of the Spirit—and know how to respond when He comes.

THE MANIFEST PRESENCE
OF THE SPIRIT

The presence of God can be expressed on several levels. First of all, God is *omnipresent*. "Omnipresence" means God is always everywhere. As Psalm 139:7-10 says, we cannot flee from God's presence. No matter where we go, He is there.

Then there is God's *indwelling presence*. When a person trusts in Jesus, the Holy Spirit comes to dwell in his or her heart. Although God is always present everywhere, He is present in the heart of the believer in a very special way. The Holy Spirit is living in you in a way that goes beyond omnipresence.

A third level of God's presence is His *manifest presence*. God manifests His presence when He chooses to reveal Himself in an *experiential* way.

What do I mean by the manifest presence of God? Think about it like this: Even as you read this book, your body is being immersed in a flood of invisible radiation. Some of this radiation is in the form of radio waves. Dozens of signals are bombarding you. Passing through your body right now are signals conveying talk shows, country music, rock music, rap music, news reports and sporting events to radios in your geographical area. But unless you have a radio turned on, you are totally unaware of their presence. These signals are all around you, but you are not experiencing them in any way. Your body is not equipped to detect those signals. That's what the omnipresence of God is like. He is always there, but with your five senses you have no way to discern Him directly.

But turn on a radio, set it at the proper frequency, and suddenly one of those invisible signals is manifested in the form of *sound*. The waves of electromagnetic radiation you could not detect on your own have been converted into a form one of your five senses can discern. Your ears can now pick up the vibrations and transmit the message to your brain. You are *experiencing* that signal.

That's what it's like when God manifests His presence—He chooses to reveal Himself in a way that can be discerned by one of your senses. You can "feel" and "sense" His presence. You can sometimes hear His voice. Sometimes there are signs of His presence you can see with your eyes. At other times there is a physical response in your body to the presence of God's mighty power.

The account of the prophet Daniel related at the beginning of this chapter is one of the most detailed descriptions in the Bible of a human being's response to God's manifest presence. (You may wish to turn to Daniel 10:4-11 and read it.) In this passage, the Spirit of God gives Daniel a vision. When the Holy Spirit came upon Daniel to communicate this vision, His presence produced an immediate physical and emotional response in those who were present.

The men with Daniel did not see the vision, but they did sense the awesome presence of God. It filled them with such fear that they ran and hid (see v. 7). And Daniel's response?

> So I was left alone, gazing at this great vision; I had no strength left, my face turned deathly pale and I was helpless. Then I heard him speaking, and as I listened to him, I fell into a deep sleep, my face to the ground. A hand touched me and set me trembling on my hands and knees (Dan. 10:8-10).

Daniel's physical response to the presence of God included a feeling of weakness, powerlessness, momentary loss of consciousness, falling to the ground, shaking and trembling. All these are common responses to the manifest presence of God. Let's look at a few other biblical accounts of what happens when God makes Himself known in this way.

The Israelites *trembled* in fear at God's presence (see Exod. 20:18-20).

Saul's soldiers *prophesied* when the Spirit came upon them. The Spirit came upon Saul, and he *lay on the ground* a day and a night *prophesying* (see 1 Sam. 19:18-24).

Isaiah *cried out in fear* at the presence of God's holiness (see Isa. 6:1-5).

Jeremiah's bones *trembled*. He was like "a drunken man, like a man overcome by wine." In the midst of this manifestation of God's presence, Jeremiah's heart was broken for God's people (see Jer. 23:9).

Ezekiel *fell to the ground* (see Ezek. 1:28—2:1).

The apostles *spoke in tongues* and *appeared to be drunk* (see Acts 2:1-13).

The apostle John *fell to the ground* as though dead (see Rev. 1:9-17).

All these—weakness, falling, trembling, "drunkenness," etc.—are physiological responses to the presence of God's omnipotent power. Our bodies are mortal and finite, and in such close proximity to God's mighty power our circuits tend to overload, sometimes producing "undignified" effects.

WHY DOES THE HOLY SPIRIT MANIFEST HIS PRESENCE?

In biblical times God manifested His presence for a number of reasons. In Luke 2:25-27, He revealed Himself to give personal revelation and direction. In Acts 10:44-46, it was to empower with the Holy Spirit and to release the gift of tongues. In 1 Samuel 10:10, He acted to equip Saul for a specific ministry and to impart the gift of prophecy. In 1 Samuel 19:18-24, He immobilized a group of soldiers so David could escape. In Luke 1:35, the Holy Spirit "overshadowed" Mary to bring about the miraculous conception of Jesus.

I've found the Holy Spirit is still working in many of these same ways today. For a number of years, I have tried to observe what takes place when the Spirit manifests His presence. While it is not always possible to discern what the Spirit is doing, I've discovered that very often the Holy Spirit manifests His presence:

1. To bring physical or emotional healing.
2. To give revelation (visions, prophecy, words of knowledge).
3. To empower for service.
4. To encourage and refresh those who are weary.
5. To attest to His presence, and assure those who are doubting.

WHEN DOES THE SPIRIT MANIFEST HIS PRESENCE?

The Holy Spirit manifests His presence whenever He chooses to do so, but there are some times when He is more likely to manifest His presence. He will often manifest Himself during a time of prayer or worship. This may be during our private devotional time or during a time of corporate worship at church.

On one occasion, I was in a large auditorium filled with 2,000 people standing and singing praises to the Lord. Suddenly, in the middle of a song, the Holy Spirit fell on that auditorium. The sense of His presence was so strong, I stopped singing right in the middle of a line. A few moments later, I noticed that everyone else had stopped singing, too. The instruments had stopped playing. The entire auditorium fell silent. For about five minutes, we stood in absolute silence. No one spoke. No one dared move.

God was there.

It was wonderful, but also a little frightening. After about five minutes, the sense of His presence lifted, and spontaneous applause rose up from 2,000 people. We entered once again into praise with a new joy. God had come and blessed us with

---

God will almost always manifest Himself when invited. Simply ask Him in faith to come, then relax and enjoy His presence.

His presence! God's presence is not always manifested in a way that is dramatic or powerful, but we can expect God will manifest His presence when we worship Him.

God will often manifest His presence when we *ask* Him to. I have found that He will almost always manifest Himself when invited (see Luke 11:13). Simply ask Him in faith to come, then relax and enjoy His presence.

Many times when I am praying for a person's healing, I will begin by asking the Holy Spirit to come upon him. When the Spirit manifests His presence, He will often simply heal the person without further prayer. Sometimes the Spirit will give me (or the person I am praying for) instructions regarding what to do next.

Many times in counseling I'll sense the Holy Spirit wants to minister to the person I'm talking with. I'll explain what I'm sensing, then ask the person I'm counseling to sit back and relax, holding his hands out, palms up, to express an attitude of receptivity. I will then put my hand on his forehead and pray out loud calmly and unemotionally for the Spirit of God to come and minister to him. Often it is a prayer as simple as "Come, Holy Spirit."

Sometimes, when I invite the Spirit to manifest Himself, very little happens at first. Often, however, there are immediate and dramatic signs of the Spirit's presence. Some time ago I was counseling a depressed individual who was contemplating suicide. Nothing I said seemed to have any effect. I asked if I could pray for the Holy Spirit to come upon him, and he gave his permission. I prayed for the Spirit to come, and the Spirit came upon him in a very gentle way. The man immediately relaxed and felt at peace; the Lord took away his desire to kill himself.

Sometimes the Spirit may remain on a person for some time. If He does, simply stay with the person and continue to pray for them either softly or silently. Sometimes you may sense that the Spirit wants to continue to work over the course of several days. In that case, instruct the person to find times to be alone with God to allow the Holy Spirit to continue His work.

HOW CAN I RECOGNIZE THE PRESENCE OF THE SPIRIT?

There is no one "sign" that will always tell you the Spirit is manifesting His presence. There are a number of things to look for, however, that will help you to learn to recognize His presence.

HOW TO RECOGNIZE WHEN THE HOLY SPIRIT IS UPON YOU

When the Holy Spirit is "upon you," He may manifest Himself in a variety of ways, including:

A feeling of heat, tingling or energy in the hands. This is often associated with an anointing for healing.

A mantle of heat on your shoulders. This is often associated with a prophetic anointing.

A "sense" of His presence. A sense that He is close, almost face-to-face with you. This is what the psalmist described when he talked about "seeking God's face."

A prompting to pray in the Spirit.

A sense of peace.

A relaxed feeling or a feeling of weakness. You may have difficulty standing. You might even fall over.

A sense that a wind is blowing against you.

A sensation like a "thickening" of the air in the room, or a change in air pressure.

A sudden loss of consciousness.

A release of emotion, a sudden uncontrollable urge to weep or laugh.

A physical response of trembling or shaking.

These signs will not always be present, but when they are, it is frequently a strong indication of His presence. Remember, when the awesome presence of God overloads the circuits of your body, it can produce strange results.

HOW TO RECOGNIZE WHEN THE
HOLY SPIRIT IS ON OTHERS

Sometimes you may recognize the presence of the Spirit on others through the spiritual gift of *discerning of spirits*. When this happens, you may see a visible "glow" around the person, or you may simply "sense" in your spirit that the Holy Spirit is upon him or her.

You can also learn to recognize a person's natural physiological response to the presence of God. These are not completely reliable, but they may be helpful when you are first learning. Signs to look for include:

A change of breathing. When you invite the Spirit to come upon someone, their breathing will often change. He or she will begin to breathe very slowly and deeply.

A quivering in the eyelids.

A feeling of heat. You can feel it radiating off of a person if you are standing close.

A sheen of perspiration on the face. It will make the person appear to be glowing if standing in a bright light.

A release of emotion, either weeping or laughing.

A physical response of trembling or shaking.

A sense of weakness, or difficulty in standing up. The person may fall over or, in rare cases, even lose consciousness.

A "look" on the person's face you will learn to recognize after a while. The person will look peaceful, happy and enthralled with the presence of God.

Again, these signs do not have to be present for the Holy Spirit to be at work, but when He is at work, these are frequently outward indications of His presence.

THE IMPORTANCE OF RECOGNIZING THE SPIRIT'S PRESENCE

When ministering to people, you always want to cooperate with what the Holy Spirit is doing. Be assured you can accomplish nothing in your own power. Developing a sensitivity to the Spirit's presence can help you to recognize and cooperate with what the Spirit is doing.

You may be walking down the street and see someone sitting on a bench with the Holy Spirit "on" them. If you see the Spirit on someone you don't know, you should pray and ask God if you are to minister to the person. It may be that he or she is under conviction of sin. God may want you to go and lead them to Jesus.

Many times in church, I will give an invitation and invite people to come forward to receive ministry. It is not unusual for twenty or thirty people to come forward. Who do I minister to first? If I were unable to recognize the presence of the Spirit, I would simply start at one end of the line and pray for people one at a time. A sensitivity to the Spirit's presence, however, gives me a second option.

When I see the line of people who have come for ministry, I look to see whom the Spirit is already on, and minister to those people first. Since the Spirit is already on them, the response is usually dramatic and apparent to all. This builds the faith level of those who are waiting for ministry. By the time I am ready to minister to them, the Holy Spirit is on them, too! This allows me to minister with far greater effectiveness.

Recognizing the presence of the Spirit can also help direct your prayers for healing. When asked to pray for someone to be healed, how do you know how long to pray? Should you just pray a quick prayer, or should you tarry in prayer until you see the healing come? One key to determining how long to pray is to see what the Holy Spirit is doing. If the Holy Spirit comes on the person with great power, you will want to continue in prayer until you are sure the Spirit has accomplished all He came to do.

Let's suppose you are praying for someone to be healed and you invite the Spirit to come upon him. Immediately, you see evidences of His presence. What do you do next?

The key is to recognize that it is the Spirit who is ministering, not you. You cannot *make* something happen. All you can do is pray into the situation and help the person respond to what God is doing. Be sensitive and available to the Spirit.

However, there are some specific things you should do when you see the Holy Spirit come upon someone you are praying for:

Listen to the Spirit. Listen for words of knowledge or directions.

Keep your eyes open. Watch the person you are ministering to. Be aware of what is happening to him or her.

Bless what God is doing. When you see evidence that God has begun to work, pray for what God is doing in that person. Pray that God would increase His power. Pray that God would continue His work. I will often pray things like this out loud: "Lord, thank You for Your presence." "I bless what You are doing in this brother right now." "Increase Your power, Lord."

Tell the person what you sense God is doing. Sometimes the person might not understand what God is doing. Share any insights God gives you. When you acknowledge God's presence, it usually will intensify. If God gives you a prophetic word, share it.

Don't hesitate to ask questions. This won't stop what God is doing. Ask, "What is God doing?" or "What are you sensing?" "Is God showing you anything?" "Is God telling you anything?" Don't spend a *lot* of time asking questions, and don't start a conversation. Give the Spirit an opportunity to do His work!

Don't be afraid to wait. If you haven't been given anything from God to say, simply wait with the person in silence, or pray softly in tongues. Don't feel like you need to be talking a lot.

Know when to stop. Feel free to stop when you sense the Holy Spirit telling you it's over, or when He appears to have completed His work. Ask the person what he felt. It's okay if he didn't feel very much happen. We can never know all that God was at work to do in those for whom we have prayed.

INVITING THE HOLY SPIRIT TO COME

During your daily time with the Lord, after you have spent time in praise, in the Word and in prayer, why not allow the Holy Spirit to come and minister to you?

Get alone in a quiet place with an attitude of worship. Sit in a comfortable chair, lean back and relax, and pray this simple prayer: "Come Holy Spirit! Come and manifest Your presence!"

Ask Him to come and heal you, refresh you, strengthen and empower you. Ask Him to speak to you and give you direction for your day.

Then relax and let Him minister to you. Don't feel like you have to keep praying. Let *Him* do it. Stay in an attitude of worship. Enjoy His presence. If He brings something to mind, write it down. The first time you do this, He may manifest Himself in a dramatic way, or you may feel very little. Just let Him minister to you as He desires. He may be doing much more than you can know.

Don't let this be a one-time event. Come back and enjoy His presence again and again. Seek time to be alone with Him. Feed on His Word. Seek His face. Talk with Him. Worship Him. He wants you to know Him, to receive His power, to see His work, to hear His voice and to fully enter into the blessings that can only be found by experiencing the Spirit.

GROUP STUDY GUIDE

Although written for individual study, this book is also useful as a study guide for small groups whose members desire a closer, more experiential walk with the Holy Spirit. The suggested group activities may be used in a Sunday School class, cell group, home Bible study or a campus small group meeting. If you are using this book for group study, each member of the group should have his or her own copy and should be encouraged to read the assigned chapter before each meeting.

SUGGESTIONS FOR THE GROUP LEADER

The purpose of this study is to lead men and women into a deeper experiential relationship with the Holy Spirit. It is not designed primarily as a Bible study or for a discussion group, although each session includes some Bible study and discussion. The overall goal is not to promote fellowship or convey information, but to encourage participants to enter into a deeper experience of the Holy Spirit and His ministries.

Depending on the church background and personal experiences of the participants, you may find a great diversity in attitudes toward the Holy Spirit. Some members of the group may have operated in the things of the Spirit for many years and come into the group with a know-it-all attitude. Others may have been taught against the work of the Spirit and consequently come to the group with a negative or critical attitude. For this reason you, as the group leader, must lead with a great deal of sensitivity. Feel free to depart from the suggested activities if you feel your group needs a different approach.

In most cases, however, those who come to your group will be genuine seekers who desire to experience a deeper relationship with the Holy Spirit. Don't automatically assume that honest concerns and questions are indications of a negative attitude or critical spirit. No matter what the background of your group members or what experiences they may have had, they can *all* experience a deeper, more meaningful walk with God if they will follow the exercises in this book with a seeking heart.

As you lead the group, try to establish an open, informal atmosphere. Give the members freedom to discuss valid concerns and questions, as long as it does not distract or divert attention from your goals for the session.

Each session should include a variety of activities. It is suggested you begin each session with a brief time of praise and worship. You may either lead on the guitar or piano, or use a prerecorded praise tape and sing along. After praise and worship, follow the suggestions given for each session, being sensitive to the Spirit's leading and the needs of the various members of the group. Many of the sessions involve breaking the group up into smaller "buzz groups." These groups should ideally be made up of between two and five people each. If your group is large, you may want to increase the number of buzz groups to maintain an ideal group size.

Each session should conclude with a time for prayer and interpersonal ministry.

Experiencing the Spirit can easily fit into a Sunday School format, taking 45 minutes to an hour. If you are doing this as a home study group, you may wish to go a little longer, but you should try to keep the sessions to less than 90 minutes. It is better to end the group session while people still want more, than to go so long that they are impatient for it to end. If you are doing a home study group, it is also suggested to have members of the group take turns bringing refreshments so you can have a brief fellowship time after each session.

WEEK #1: WHO IS THIS HOLY SPIRIT?

PREPARATION

Have everyone in the group read the introduction and chapter 1 of *Experiencing the Spirit*.

INTRODUCTION

Begin by having the group members share what they think of when they hear the words "Holy Spirit." Listen carefully to the answers. This is a crucial time to determine the background and attitudes of your group members. If the members of your group answer with a trite "theological" answer like "the third person of the Trinity," probe a little deeper. What do they think the Holy Spirit is like? How do they think He wants to relate to them?

Try to determine what experiences the members of your group have had with the Holy Spirit. Are they enthusiastic about experiencing the Spirit, or are they uncertain and fearful? Be aware that there may be some in your group who have long been taught against seeking experiences with the Spirit.

If some in the group are negative or critical in their attitudes, you will need to be very careful in dealing with them. If you find they distract or divert the group from the goal of learning to experience the Spirit, you may need to meet with them privately and explain the purpose of the group. Explain that while their questions and concerns may be valid topics for discussion, the purpose of this group is to aid those who are seeking a deeper experience with the Holy Spirit. If they are not able to suspend their disbelief and critical attitudes long enough to do this, it would be better for them not to attend the group.

As you begin the session, explain why you desire to lead a study of *Experiencing the Spirit*. Take four or five minutes to share a brief testimony of what the Holy Spirit has done in your life. Briefly review the material in the chapter and allow a brief time for discussion. This review should not be an in-depth teaching. Take about 10 minutes to cover the main points of the chapter and share any personal experiences you have had that may be helpful as illustrations.

Keep an eye on your watch during the discussion time and don't let it drag on. Depending on the time available, 10 minutes should be the maximum.

GROUP ACTIVITY

Introduce the activity with something like this: "The Bible uses a number of symbols to describe the Holy Spirit. Some of these include fire (see Isa. 4:4; Matt. 3:11; Acts 2), wind (see Ezek. 37:7-20), water (see John 7:38,39), oil (see Acts 10:38; 1 John 2:27) and a dove (see Matt. 3:16). To gain a better understanding of these symbols, let's brainstorm a little."

Divide into three groups and assign each group one of the three symbols on the study sheet. Have them brainstorm together for about 10 minutes, and then have each group share their conclusions.

When all three groups have shared, ask, "What do these three symbols have in common?" and "How are these symbols different?" Conclude by summing up what you think God is teaching us through the use of these symbols.

Introduce next week's chapter and conclude the meeting with a time of prayer.

GROUP STUDY SHEET — WEEK #1

GROUP ONE: THE HOLY SPIRIT AS FIRE
(Isa. 4:4, Matt. 3:11, Acts 2:3)

THINK ABOUT THE SIGNIFICANCE
OF FIRE AS A SYMBOL.

What are the uses of fire?

What are the values of fire?

What are the dangers of fire?

What do you think God is trying to tell us about the Holy
Spirit by picturing Him as fire?

GROUP TWO: THE HOLY SPIRIT AS WIND
(Ezek. 37:7-10; John 3:8; Acts 2:1,2)

THINK ABOUT THE SIGNIFICANCE
OF WIND AS A SYMBOL.

What are the uses of wind?

What are the values of wind?

What are the dangers of wind?

What do you think God is trying to tell us about the Holy Spirit by picturing Him as wind?

GROUP THREE: THE HOLY SPIRIT AS WATER
(John 4:14; John 7:38,39)

THINK ABOUT THE SIGNIFICANCE
OF WATER AS A SYMBOL.

What are the uses of water?

What are the values of water?

What are the dangers of water?

What do you think God is trying to tell us about the Holy Spirit by picturing Him as water?

WEEK #2: THE INDWELLING SPIRIT

PREPARATION

Have everyone in the group read chapter 2 of *Experiencing the Spirit*.

INTRODUCTION

Briefly review the material in the chapter and ask if there are any questions. Allow a brief time for discussion. This review should not be an in-depth teaching. Take about 15 minutes to cover the main points of the chapter.

Share ways you have seen the Holy Spirit change your life as you have walked with the Lord. Give others an opportunity to share briefly how the indwelling Spirit has changed their lives. Keep an eye on your watch during the discussion time and don't let it drag on. Depending on the time available, 20 minutes should be the maximum.

GROUP ACTIVITY

Divide into two groups and give each group one of the two study guides provided. Have each group work through their study guide together, then try to summarize what they found. Meet back together and have each group share what they found. Allow time for any questions or discussion, then summarize the importance of the Spirit's indwelling ministry.

Introduce next week's chapter and conclude the meeting with a time of prayer.

GROUP STUDY SHEET — WEEK #2

GROUP ONE: INDWELLING AND EMPOWERING
The indwelling ministry of the Spirit is prophesied in the Old Testament Scriptures. Read each of the following passages and write down what was to be the result when God placed His Spirit within His people:

Ezekiel 11:18-20 _____

Ezekiel 36:25-27 _____

The empowering ministry of the Spirit is also described in the Old Testament. (The empowering of the Spirit is usually described as God pouring out His Spirit on His people, rather than into them.) Read the following passages and write down what effect is produced when God pours out His Spirit on His people:

Numbers 11:25,26 _____

Isaiah 44:3-5 _____

Joel 2:28 _____

In light of these passages, summarize in your own words the difference between the Spirit's indwelling ministry and His empowering ministry.

GROUP TWO: THE INDWELLING SPIRIT
The following verses describe the indwelling ministry of the Holy Spirit. Look up each verse and write down what impresses you about the indwelling work of the Spirit.

John 14:16,17 _____

John 14:26 _____

Rom. 8:4-6 _____

Rom. 8:11-16 _____

2 Cor. 1:21,22 _____

Summarize in your own words what you have discovered about the indwelling ministry of the Spirit.

WEEK #3: TRANSFORMED BY THE SPIRIT

PREPARATION

Have everyone in the group read chapter 3 of *Experiencing the Spirit*.

INTRODUCTION

Briefly review the material in the chapter and ask if there are any questions. Allow a brief time for discussion. This review should not be an extended teaching. Take about 15 minutes to cover the main points of the chapter and share any personal experiences you have had that may be helpful as illustrations. Keep an eye on your watch during the discussion time and don't let it drag on. Depending on your time available, 15 minutes should be the maximum.

GROUP ACTIVITY

Introduce the activity this way: "If we're going to fill our minds with God's Word, it's important we know how to study and apply it. Let's take, as a sample passage, Romans 8:12-16. We'll spend a few minutes studying the passage, then share our results with each other."

Make copies of the study sheet for each person in the group. Pass out the sheets and give the members about 20 minutes to study the passage. Go through the sheets together and allow individuals to share what they have written for each question.

Suggest that in their personal quiet times, participants take a different passage each day to study through in this way. It is crucial to feed on the Word and allow the Spirit to apply it to our lives daily.

Introduce next week's chapter and conclude the meeting with a time of prayer.

GROUP STUDY SHEET — WEEK #3

STEP ONE: PRAY AND ASK THE HOLY SPIRIT TO GIVE YOU UNDERSTANDING.

STEP TWO: READ ROMANS 8:12-16.

Therefore, brothers, we have an obligation—but it is not to the sinful nature, to live according to it. For if you live according to the sinful nature, you will die; but if by the Spirit you put to death the misdeeds of the body, you will live, because those who are led by the Spirit of God are sons of God. For you did not receive a spirit that makes you a slave again to fear, but you received the Spirit of sonship. And by him we cry, "Abba, Father." The Spirit himself testifies with our spirit that we are God's children (Rom. 8:12-16).

STEP THREE: QUESTIONS FOR UNDERSTANDING

1. What most impressed me in this passage?

2. What questions does this passage bring to mind?

3. What new lesson did I learn from this passage?

4. How should this passage change the way I act, think or feel?

WEEK #4: EQUIPPED TO SERVE

PREPARATION
Have everyone in the group read chapter 4 of *Experiencing the Spirit.*

INTRODUCTION
Briefly review the material in the chapter and ask if there are any questions. Allow a brief time for discussion. This review should not be an extended teaching. Take about 15 minutes to cover the main points of the chapter and share any personal experiences you have had that may be helpful as illustrations. For your personal study, you may wish to skip ahead and review the material in chapter 5 before you teach the session. This will help you to know where the study is going.

Keep an eye on your watch during the discussion time and don't let it drag on. Depending on your time available, 15 minutes should be the maximum.

GROUP ACTIVITY
Choose one or more of the following options, depending on the time available:

OPTION ONE: Testimonies of the Spirit's Power
Introduce this activity this way: "God still works in power today, just as He did in New Testament times. Most people who have been Christians for more than a few years have had experiences where they know God worked supernaturally to heal, protect or provide for them. Take a few moments and try to think of a time when the Holy Spirit worked supernaturally in your life."

As group leader, share a supernatural experience with the

Spirit from your own life, and then have open discussion for a few minutes, so that others can give their testimonies. Try to keep each testimony under five minutes. As they share their experiences, try to encourage and affirm them.

OPTION TWO: Empowering in the Old Testament and the New *Use this option if time is limited.* Have the members read 1 Samuel 10:1-11 and review Numbers 11:10-27. Ask, "What elements does 1 Samuel 10:1-11 have in common with Numbers 11:10-27? How are the two experiences with the Spirit different? How are these experiences similar to the experience of the apostles in Acts 2? How are they different?"

OPTION THREE: Empowering in the Old Testament and the New *Use this option if time is available for a longer study.* Divide into two groups. Have the groups look up the Bible passages on the next page and answer the questions about the empowering ministry of the Spirit. Bring the groups back together and have a spokesperson from each group share what the group found.

Sum up what this chapter is teaching about the empowering of the Spirit. Introduce next week's chapter and conclude the meeting with a time of prayer.

GROUP STUDY SHEET—WEEK #4

GROUP ONE:
Look up the following passages and write down in a few words what was taking place in each one. Then answer the questions about the Spirit's empowering ministry:

Num. 11:16-29

Judges 3:9-11

1 Sam. 10:1-11

Acts 2:1-13

Acts 4:29-31

What similar elements do you find repeated in the above passages?

How were the experiences in the Old Testament passages similar to the experience of the apostles in the book of Acts?

How were the Old Testament experiences different from the New Testament experiences?

GROUP TWO:

Look up the following passages and write down in a few words what was taking place in each one, then answer the questions about the Spirit's empowering ministry:

Num. 24:2-5

1 Sam. 19:19-24

Joel 2:28

Acts 2:1-13

Acts 4:29-31

What similar elements do you find repeated in the above passages?

How were the experiences in the Old Testament passages similar to the experience of the apostles in the book of Acts?

How were the Old Testament experiences different from the New Testament experiences?

WEEK #5: RECEIVING HIS POWER

PREPARATION
Have everyone in the group read chapter 5 of *Experiencing the Spirit*.

INTRODUCTION
Briefly review the material in the chapter, and ask if there are any questions. Allow a brief time for discussion. This review should not be an extended teaching. Take about 15 minutes to cover the main points of the lesson. Keep an eye on your watch during the discussion time and don't let it drag on. Depending on your time available, 15 minutes should be the maximum.

GROUP ACTIVITY
It's always interesting to see how various individuals came into the experience of the empowering of the Spirit. Give your own testimony of how you were filled with the Spirit. You may wish to have others share their testimonies, too.

Divide into two small groups and have each group work through the following study sheet. Then bring the groups back together to share what they found.

Explain the need to constantly recharge our spiritual batteries. If any of the members of the group have never been filled, or if some of them need a "fresh touch," have a time to pray for them to be filled. Have the person desiring prayer sit in a chair in the middle of the room. Follow the instructions in the chapter. If you have not prayed to impart the filling of the Holy Spirit before, you may also wish to review chapter 12.

Sum up what this chapter is teaching about the empowering of the Spirit. Introduce next week's chapter and conclude the meeting with a time of prayer.

GROUP STUDY SHEET — WEEK #5

Read the following passages from the book of Acts. Each passage records an incident in which people received the empowering of the Spirit. Next to each reference, write down who was empowered, what, if anything, the people did to receive it, and what outward evidence of the empowering was present.

GROUP ONE:

Acts 1:13,14; 2:1-4

Acts 4:31

Acts 8:14-19

What most impressed you as you studied these passages?

GROUP TWO:

Acts 9:10-17

Acts 10:44-47

Acts 19:6

What most impressed you as you studied these passages?

WEEK #6:
DOING THE WORK OF THE KINGDOM

PREPARATION
Have everyone in the group read chapter 6 of *Experiencing the Spirit*.

INTRODUCTION
Briefly review the material in the chapter, and ask if there are any questions. Allow a brief time for discussion. This review should not be an extended teaching. Take about 15 minutes to cover the main points of the chapter and share any personal experiences you have had that may be helpful as illustrations.

GROUP ACTIVITY
OPTION ONE: In preparation for the session, collect a number of copies of your daily newspaper from recent weeks. Introduce the activity by saying something like this: "Who can remember from the book some of the things that characterize Satan's kingdom?" Encourage a response. Have them list as many of the elements as they can.

"What are the things that characterize God's kingdom?" Again, have them list as many of the characteristics as they can.

"The apostle John wrote that the whole world lies in the power of the evil one. Today I want us to see what that means in very practical terms. Let's take a few minutes and look through the front page of our city's newspaper." Give each person a front page from your local paper. If possible, give them each a paper from a different day of the week. "I want to make a list of all of the evidences from our newspaper that

Satan's kingdom is being manifested in our city (or county, nation, world)."

Take a sheet of paper and write at the top, "Evidence of Satan's Kingdom." Have the members of the group go through the papers and tell you the various reported events that indicate Satan's will is being accomplished.

Now take a sheet of paper and write down "Evidence of God's Kingdom." Have them look through the papers to see if there is any evidence God's kingdom is being manifested in your area.

"God wants us to see that our cities and nations are under the domination of Satan. His charge to us is to pray that in the midst of this darkness, the power of God would be manifested, that His kingdom would come and His will be done in this place."

Go into a time of prayer and pray specifically for your city and nation, that the will of God would be done and His kingdom manifested where you live. Be specific in your prayers.

OPTION TWO: Break up into groups of two as prayer and study partners and study through the following study sheet together, writing down the areas of ministry God wants His people to be equipped to do. Have each person then choose which area they most strongly desire to serve God in. Have them pray for each other in these areas. Then bring the group back together and share any insights God gave.

Sum up what this chapter is teaching about ministry in the Spirit. Introduce next week's chapter and conclude the meeting with a time of prayer.

GROUP STUDY SHEET — WEEK #6

MINISTRIES GOD WANTS TO GIVE HIS PEOPLE
Study through the following passages together, writing down
the areas of ministry in which God wants His people to serve.

Mark 16:15-18

John 14:12

Acts 1:8

1 Cor. 14:1-5

1 Thess. 5:11

Hebrews 5:12

In which of these areas of ministry do you most desire to see
God use you?

WEEK #7: WALKING IN THE ANOINTING

PREPARATION

Have everyone in the group read chapter 7 of *Experiencing the Spirit*.

INTRODUCTION

Briefly review the material in the chapter and ask if there are any questions. Allow a brief time for discussion. This review should not be an extended teaching. Take about 20 minutes to cover the main points of the chapter and share any personal experiences you have had that may be helpful as illustrations. Keep an eye on your watch during the discussion time and don't let it drag on. Depending on your time available, 20 minutes should be the maximum.

GROUP ACTIVITY

Divide into two groups and study through the following study sheets together. Then come together and share your findings.

Make a list of people you know who are in various kinds of need. If any members of your group share personal needs, stop and pray for them right away. When your list is complete, spend some time praying through it together. Ask the members of the group to pray for each of the people in need daily during the course of the week and to be sensitive to any promptings from the Spirit to minister at the point of these needs.

Introduce next week's chapter and conclude the meeting with prayer.

Answer Key: A-3, B-1, C-5, D-2, E-4

GROUP STUDY SHEET — WEEK #7

GROUP ONE: THE MINISTRY OF JESUS

Read the following account of Jesus' sermon in Luke 4:16-21. In this passage Jesus announced that His earthly ministry was a fulfillment of five specific elements of Isaiah's prophecy. Read through the passages listed in the right-hand column. Which element of Isaiah's prophecy is fulfilled in each of these passages? Write the number of the relevant prophecy in the blank next to the verse.

He went to Nazareth, where he had been brought up, and on the Sabbath day he went into the synagogue, as was his custom. And he stood up to read. The scroll of the prophet Isaiah was handed to him. Unrolling it, he found the place where it is written: "The Spirit of the Lord is on me, because he has anointed me

A. Luke 18:42 _____

B. Luke 4:43,44 _____

C. Luke 5:20 _____

D. Luke 4:33-36 _____

E. Luke 4:33-36 _____

[1] to preach good news [the Gospel] to the poor. He has sent me

[2] to proclaim freedom for the prisoners [those held captive by demonic forces]

[3] and recovery of sight for the [physically and spiritually] blind,

[4] to release the oppressed [suffering various forms of affliction and pain],

[5] to proclaim the year of the Lord's favor [the year of Jubilee, when all debts are forgiven]." Then he rolled up the scroll, gave it back to the attendant and sat down. The eyes of everyone in the synagogue were fastened on him, and he began by saying to them, "Today this scripture is fulfilled in your hearing."

As you walk in the anointing, how might God use you to fulfill these five aspects of Jesus' ministry? Give specific examples.

GROUP TWO: THE POWER OF GOD IN MINISTRY
Look up the following passages and summarize what each says about the power of God in ministry:

Isaiah 61:1-3

Luke 24:49

Acts 1:8

Acts 10:38

Romans 15:17-19

1 Corinthians 2:4,5

1 Corinthians 4:20

Based on your study of these passages, sum up in your own words what the Bible teaches about the power of God in ministry.

WEEK #8: THE GIFTS OF THE SPIRIT

PREPARATION
Have everyone in the group read chapter 8 of *Experiencing the Spirit.*

INTRODUCTION
Briefly review the material in the chapter and ask if there are any questions. Be sure to cover the motivational gifts. Share any personal experiences you have had that may be helpful as illustrations. Allow a brief time for discussion.

As a group leader, you will need to exercise a great deal of sensitivity concerning the section on spiritual gifts. Some of the members of your group may have been taught that the gifts of the Holy Spirit are no longer in operation. If there are questions about this, an excellent resource is Jack Deere's *Surprised by the Power of the Spirit* (Zondervan). The author does an excellent job of dealing with the "cessationist" arguments from a biblical and theological standpoint.

I would not suggest devoting time to the discussion of this issue unless (1) someone in the group brings it up and (2) it is a topic most of the group is concerned about. The best way to "prove" the existence of the gifts is not by theological argument, but by allowing the group members to see them in operation and to personally experience them.

GROUP ACTIVITY
OPTION ONE: Motivational Gifts
Introduce the activity this way: "If each of us has been given a motivational gift from God, we should be able to figure out what gift we have and recognize the giftings of others. Let's see if we can recognize each other's motivational gift."

Give each individual a stack of index cards equal to the number of members in the group. For example, if your group has ten members, give each member ten index cards. Have each member write the name of a different group member on each card and next to the name write down the motivational gift they think that person has. Each member will be writing down what gift he or she thinks each of the other members have. This activity will be more profitable if the members of the group know each other well, but it can still be helpful if they have only known each other a few weeks.

Give the members a few minutes to do this, then have them give each person all the cards with his or her name on them. Go around the room and have each person read the gifts various people thought they had. Ask if there are any surprises.

Encourage the group members to follow the motivational gifts God has given them so that they can reach out and do the works of Jesus!

OPTION TWO: Ministry Gifts

Review the nine ministry gifts, then share something like this: "In 1 Corinthians 14:1 God exhorts us to 'eagerly desire' or 'covet' spiritual gifts. What does it mean to eagerly desire something? Who can think of something you have eagerly desired in the last year? What do you do when you eagerly desire or covet something?

"God wants us to desire His gifts; to seek after them; to 'press in' and pursue them until we are proficient in them. It's not wrong to want more and greater gifts. Gifts are not a badge of superiority, they are tools that allow us to serve God more effectively. One way we are released into the operation of a spiritual gift is by the laying on of hands. The Bible teaches that as we lay hands on each other and pray for each other, spiritual gifts are released and imparted." (See Rom. 1:11; 1 Tim. 4:14; 2 Tim. 1:6.)

Ask for a volunteer who would like the group to pray over him or her that a spiritual gift may be imparted. Have the volunteer sit in a chair in the middle of the group. Have other members of the group lay hands on him or her and agree with you in prayer for the impartation of the desired gift. If you have not led a group in this kind of ministry before, you may wish to review the material in chapter 12 before this session.

You may wish to allow this to flow into a general ministry time when you lay hands on the sick and pray for healing, share prophetic insights, etc.

Introduce next week's chapter and conclude the meeting with prayer.

WEEK #9: PRAYING IN THE SPIRIT

PREPARATION
Have everyone in the group read chapter 9 of *Experiencing the Spirit*.

INTRODUCTION
Briefly review the material in the chapter and ask if there are any questions. Allow a brief time for discussion. Take about 20 minutes to cover the main points of the chapter and share any personal experiences you have had that may be helpful as illustrations. As in the last chapter, you will need to exercise a great deal of sensitivity concerning the section on tongues. Please note the cautions and suggestions given in chapter 8.

GROUP ACTIVITY
Divide into two groups. Have the first group study 1 Cor. 14:1-28 and write down any cautions, limitations or *negative* statements about the gift of tongues. Have the other group study the same passage and write down the *positive* statements about tongues. Give the groups about 15 minutes to do this, then have them share their results. From what we see in this passage, what is the biblical attitude toward this gift?

Encourage members of the group who speak in tongues to share how they entered into the gift. You may also share your own testimony if you speak in tongues.

If any of the group would like prayer to have the gift of tongues released, pray for them, but be careful not to pressure anyone. Many times tongues are released when a person is alone with God and feels less inhibited.

Sum up what this chapter is teaching about praying in the Spirit. Introduce next week's chapter and conclude the meeting with a time of prayer.

WEEK #10: REVELATION BY THE SPIRIT

PREPARATION
Have everyone in the group read chapter 10 of *Experiencing the Spirit*.

INTRODUCTION
Briefly review the material in the chapter and ask if there are any questions. Allow a brief time for discussion. Take about 15 minutes to cover the main points of the chapter. Share a testimony of an occasion when you have heard the voice of God and the positive fruit the encounter has since produced in your life.

GROUP ACTIVITY
Explain that you are going to ask the Spirit of God to release His prophetic revelation in the group. Choose three or four of the more mature members of the group to assist you. They will form what is called a "prophetic presbytery." They will try to hear and release what God is saying to a few individuals from the group.

Ask for a volunteer, or choose someone you feel will be receptive to be the first one the presbytery will prophesy to. Have the person who will receive prophecy sit in a chair. Position the chairs for those who will prophesy so they are facing the person they are ministering to.

Remind those who will prophesy that they have the "mind of Christ." Prophetic words do not always come from the outside. Prophecy often comes as a sensing in your spirit of what the Holy Spirit is saying to the person.

Remind them that the purpose of personal prophecy is to strengthen, to encourage and to comfort (see 1 Cor. 14:3).

Give the following directions to those who will be prophesying:

1. Look (the person's name) in the eye.
2. Begin to pray softly in tongues. This will sensitize your spirit to hear what God is saying.
3. Ask God to reveal to you what He would say to (the person's name) that would strengthen, encourage and comfort him (or her).
4. Speak in a normal tone of voice. Introduce what you are saying with something like, "I believe the Lord would say to you..."

Each member of the presbytery is free to prophesy as the Holy Spirit leads. Allow the prophecy to go on for four or five minutes or until it seems that nothing more is forthcoming.

If someone gets off track and begins to give reproof, correction or specific direction, you need to gently interrupt them and remind them that the purpose of New Testament prophetic ministry is to strengthen, encourage and comfort.

If appropriate, ask the person who received prophecy if God spoke to him or her through what was said.

Ask who would like to receive ministry next. After several have been ministered to, briefly review the importance of seeking the gift of prophecy.

Briefly introduce the next chapter, then close the meeting in prayer that God would increase the prophetic gifting of each member of the group.

WEEK #11: THE GIFTS OF HEALING

PREPARATION
Have everyone in the group read chapter 11 of *Experiencing the Spirit.*

INTRODUCTION
Briefly review the material in the chapter and ask if there are any questions. Share a testimony of an occasion when you have experienced God's healing power. Be sure to describe what you felt and what fruit resulted. Give the group members an opportunity to share testimonies of occasions when they have experienced God's healing.

GROUP ACTIVITY
Explain that it's not enough to *know about* healing. God wants us to see the sick *healed.* Ask if anyone in the group would like prayer for healing. In most groups there will be a number of people with some level of physical infirmity.

Review the five steps given at the end of chapter 11 for praying for the sick. Place a chair in the center of the group and have those who want prayer for healing sit in it one at a time, while the others gather around and pray.

Invite the Holy Spirit to come and release His healing power. Have the group members lay hands on the sick person and pray as the Spirit leads. If you sense something happening, ask the individual receiving prayer what he or she experienced.

Pray for all of the members of the group who desire prayer.

Introduce next week's chapter and close with prayer, thanking God for what He has done.

WEEK #12: THE MANIFEST PRESENCE OF THE SPIRIT

PREPARATION
Have everyone in the group read chapter 12 of *Experiencing the Spirit*.

INTRODUCTION
Briefly review the material in the chapter and ask if there are any questions. Allow a brief time for discussion. Share a testimony of an occasion when you have experienced the presence of God in a powerful way. Be sure to describe what you felt and what fruit resulted. Give the group members an opportunity to share testimonies of occasions when they have sensed God's presence.

GROUP ACTIVITY
OPTION ONE: Divide into two groups and work through the study sheet. Then come together and discuss their responses.

OPTION TWO: Introduce the activity like this: "Tonight we want to ask the Holy Spirit to come and manifest His presence right here."

Have everyone sit back and relax. Tell them not to get tense or try to make something happen. Encourage them not to keep asking or praying, but to simply allow God to do what He desires to do. You may want to play a tape of soft praise music in the background, but this is not essential.

You, as leader, should pray and invite the presence of the Holy Spirit to come. It can be a very simple prayer like, "Come,

Holy Spirit! Come and manifest Your presence. Release the flow of Your power. Come and minister to Your people!" After you have prayed, wait quietly for several minutes to give the Spirit time to work.

Keep your eyes open and look to see whom the Holy Spirit is ministering to. Usually the Spirit will begin ministering to one or two right away. If you don't sense anything happening, just wait on the Lord.

If you see signs of the Spirit's work, point out whom the Spirit is on and encourage the others to continue waiting on the Lord. Often there is an initial "wave" of the Spirit ministering to a few, and then five or ten minutes later another wave of the Spirit will sweep across the group. The Spirit might not choose to minister to everyone on any one occasion. Let Him minister as He wills.

When you see the Holy Spirit on someone, go and lay your hand on him or her and pray. You can either pray for the person softly in tongues, share any encouraging prophetic word the Lord gives you, or simply lay your hand on his or her head and pray something like, "Lord, thank You for Your presence on this one. Do a deep work, Lord. Increase Your anointing."

After praying for those the Spirit is on, pray over the group and ask the Holy Spirit to release more of His power on them. Encourage the members to continue waiting, allowing the Spirit to work. As you continue to wait on the Lord, go back again and pray over those the Spirit is on. Ask the Spirit to continue His work, to pour out His blessing, to touch the person deeply.

After 15 to 20 minutes, or as the Spirit leads, close the time in prayer. Ask those the Spirit was on to share what they experienced.

Conclude the meeting with prayer, thanking God for what He has done!

GROUP STUDY SHEET — WEEK #12

WHEN THE SPIRIT MANIFESTS HIS PRESENCE
Read the following passages and note the response of the people to God's manifest presence.

GROUP ONE:

    Exodus 20:18-20

    1 Samuel 19:18-24

    Isaiah 6:1-5

    Jeremiah 23:9

    Acts 9:3-5

What most impressed you in these passages?

GROUP TWO:

    Genesis 17:3

    Ezekiel 1:28–2:1

    John 18:4-6

    Acts 2:1-13

Revelation 1:9-17

What most impressed you in these passages?

ENDNOTES

CHAPTER ONE

1. Jack W. Hayford, *The Power and the Blessing: Celebrating the Disciplines of Spirit-Filled Living* (Colorado Springs: Victor Books, 1994), p. 21.
2. Bill Bright, *The Holy Spirit: The Key to Supernatural Living* (San Bernardino: Here's Life Publishers, Inc., 1980), pp. 116, 121.
3. Don Stewart, *95 Questions People Ask About the Holy Spirit* (Wheaton: Tyndale House Publishers, 1987), p. 17.
4. Ibid., p. 19.
5. V. R. Edam, ed., *Crisis Experience in the Lives of Noted Christians* (Minneapolis: Bethany Fellowship, Inc.), pp. 63, 64.
6. Merill F. Unger, *Demons in the World Today: A Study of Occultism in the Light of God's Word* (Wheaton: Tyndale House Publishers, 1971), pp. 130-133.
7. C. H. Spurgeon, "The Power of the Holy Ghost." A sermon delivered at New Park Street Chapel, Southwark on Sunday, June 17, 1855. The Spurgeon Archive, Sermon Number 30, http://www.spurgeon.org/sermons/0030.html, pp. 11, 12.

CHAPTER TWO

1. John F. Walvoord, *The Holy Spirit* (Grand Rapids: Zondervan Publishing House, 1958), p. 136.
2. C. I. Scofield, *Scofield Reference Bible* (New York: Oxford University Press, 1945), p. 1247.

CHAPTER FOUR

1. C. Peter Wagner, *Praying with Power* (Ventura: Regal Books, 1997), pp. 120, 121.

2. Alex Buchan, "Signs and Wonders in China," *Charisma*, January 1998, p. 38.

CHAPTER FIVE
1. Garnet E. Pike, *Receiving the Promise of the Father: How to Be Baptized in the Holy Spirit* (Franklin Springs: LifeSprings Resources, 1997), pp. 19-21.

CHAPTER SIX
1. John Wimber with Kevin Springer, *Power Evangelism* (San Francisco: Harper & Row, Publishers, 1986), p. 14.

CHAPTER SEVEN
1. Kenneth E. Hagin, *Understanding the Anointing* (Tulsa: Rhema Bible Church, 1983), p. 124.

CHAPTER EIGHT
1. *Strong's Greek-Hebrew Dictionary* (Seattle: Biblesoft and International Bible Translators, Inc., 1994). Included in "The PC Study Bible Version Two for Windows, Complete Reference Library," Strong's Greek Definition #5486.
2. Kevin J. Conner, *The Church in the New Testament* (Portland: City Bible Publishing, 1989), p. 214.
3. Owen Weston, *Your Job Description from God: Spiritual Gifts, A Guide for the Development of Lay Ministries* (Franklin Springs: LifeSprings Resources, 1996), p. 95.
4. Ibid., p. 97.
5. C. Peter Wagner, *Your Spiritual Gifts Can Help Your Church Grow* (Ventura: Regal Books, 1994), p. 146.
6. Leslie B. Flynn, *Nineteen Gifts of the Spirit: Which Do You*

Have? Are You Using Them? (Colorado Springs: Victor Books, 1974), p. 170.

7. Frank Damazio, *The Making of a Leader* (Portland: Trilogy Productions, 1988), p. 49.

8. R. M. Riggs, *The Spirit Himself* (Springfield: Gospel Publishing House, 1949), p. 148.

9. Wagner, *Your Spiritual Gifts Can Help Your Church Grow*, p. 200.

10. Damazio, *The Making of a Leader*, p. 50.

11. Ibid.

12. Bruce Bugbee, *Networking* (Leader's Guide) (Pasadena: Charles E. Fuller Institute of Evangelism and Church Growth, 1989), p. 53.

CHAPTER TEN

1. Wayne A. Grudem, "Why Christians Can Still Prophesy," *Christianity Today*, 16 September 1988, p. 35.

2. Ibid.

3. Charles Caldwell Ryrie, *The Ryrie Study Bible: New American Standard Translation* (Chicago: Moody Press, 1976), p. 1744.

4. C. F. Keil and F. Delitzsch, *Commentary on the Old Testament in Ten Volumes*, Vol. III (Grand Rapids: William B. Eerdmans Publishing Company), p. 290.

CHAPTER ELEVEN

1. John F. Walvoord, *The Holy Spirit* (Grand Rapids: Zondervan Publishing House, 1958), p. 180.

For information on scheduling Robert Heidler for
a retreat or conference, or to receive a free copy of his ministry
newsletter, please contact:

Glory of Zion Outreach Ministries
P.O. Box 598
Denton, Texas 76202
Phone: (940) 382-1166
Fax: (940) 565-9264
Email: believer@iglobal.net

Six More Ways to Experience the Spirit

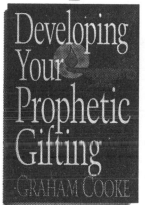

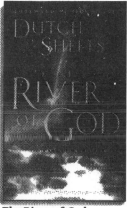

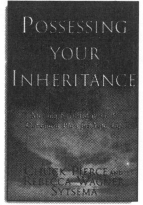

The Sword of the Spirit
S E R I E S

A School of Ministry in the Word & the Spirit *By Colin Dye*

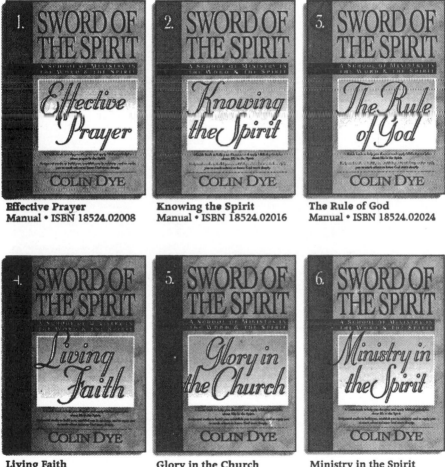

Effective Prayer
Manual • ISBN 18524.02008

Knowing the Spirit
Manual • ISBN 18524.02016

The Rule of God
Manual • ISBN 18524.02024

Living Faith
Manual • ISBN 18524.02032

Glory in the Church
Manual • ISBN 18524.02040

Ministry in the Spirit
Manual • ISBN 18524.02059